JUST RELATIONSHIPS

Bringing a social justice lens to daily interpersonal relationships, *Just Relationships* offers a perspective on existing social science theory that demonstrates how our personal relationships should be grounded in fairness and justice. Douglas Kelley utilizes concepts from a variety of academic disciplines and helping professions to examine the barriers encountered in achieving balanced partnerships. This student-friendly book brings the important new perspective of social justice to courses focusing on interpersonal relationships and family relationships, supplementing traditional textbooks. This book presents key relationship theories in each chapter and then applies them from a social justice perspective; uses thought-provoking case studies and guiding questions to enhance student learning; examines a number of different types of interpersonal relationships including family, friends, lovers, and mentor-mentee relationships within a variety of socioeconomic and sociocultural contexts.

Douglas Kelley's work focuses on interpersonal communication processes, especially as they relate to forgiveness, intimacy, and love. A Professor of Communication Studies at Arizona State University (where he received the Centennial Professor Award), Kelley teaches relationship-based courses such as Family Communication, Relational Communication, Conflict and Negotiation, Forgiveness and Reconciliation, and Inner-City Families. He is a frequent speaker regarding marriage and family communication, conflict, and forgiveness at various community groups, including local schools and organizations working to break the cycle of generational poverty, and has presented his ideas in the Middle East. He has served on the editorial board for the *Journal of Family Communication* and has published in such outlets as the *Journal of Social and Personal Relationships*, and *Human Communication Research*. Find out more about Kelley and his work at RelationshipArt.com.

JUST RELATIONSHIPS

Living Out Social Justice as Mentor, Family, Friend, and Lover

Douglas L. Kelley

Routledge
Taylor & Francis Group

NEW YORK AND LONDON

First published 2017
by Routledge
711 Third Avenue, New York, NY 10017

and by Routledge
2 Park Square, Milton Park, Abingdon, Oxon, OX14 4RN

Routledge is an imprint of the Taylor & Francis Group, an informa business

© 2017 Taylor & Francis

Library of Congress Cataloging-in-Publication Data
Names: Kelley, Douglas L., author.
Title: Just relationships : living out social justice as mentor, family, friend and lover / Douglas Kelley.
Description: New York, NY : Routledge, 2017. | Includes bibliographical references and index.
Identifiers: LCCN 2016019403 (print) | LCCN 2016041835 (ebook) | ISBN 9781629580586 (hardback) | ISBN 9781629580593 (pbk.) | ISBN 9781315452258 (ebook)
Subjects: LCSH: Interpersonal relations—Moral and ethical aspects. | Social justice.
Classification: LCC HM1106 .K446 2017 (print) | LCC HM1106 (ebook) | DDC 302—dc23
LC record available at https://lccn.loc.gov/2016019403

ISBN: 978-1-629-58058-6 (hbk)
ISBN: 978-1-629-58059-3 (pbk)
ISBN: 978-1-315-45225-8 (ebk)

Typeset in Garamond
by Apex CoVantage, LLC

With much thanks to Kit
And all the staff and kids and families at Neighborhood Ministries

Blessed are those who hunger and thirst for righteousness . . .
Blessed are the merciful . . .
Blessed are the pure in heart . . .
Blessed are the peacemakers . . .

—Jesus

Most people are afraid of suffering. But suffering is a kind of mud to help the lotus flower of happiness grow. There can be no lotus flower without the mud.

—Thich Nhat Hanh

One may stand perplexed before some thought, especially seeing men's sin, asking oneself: "Shall I take it by force, or by humble love?" Always resolve to take it by humble love. If you so resolve once and for all, you will be able to overcome the whole world. A loving humility is a terrible power, the most powerful of all, nothing compares with it.

—Dostoevsky

CONTENTS

Acknowledgments   ix
Foreword by Valerie Manusov   xi
Preface   xiv
Cases and Concepts   xvii

PART I
Imagining Just Relationships: Perspectives   1

1 Just Thoughts   3

2 Just Relationships   9

3 Good Relationships   19

4 Love Relationships   30

5 Interpersonal Advocacy: Creating Spaces   40

PART II
Barriers to Just Relationships: Perceptions That Separate   53

6 Worldview: Your Relationship Frame   55

7 Dehumanizing the "Other"   67

8 Saving Face   76

9 Shame on You, Shame on Me   85

PART III
Shaping Just Relationships: Creating a Just Future   95

10 Resilience: Ordinary Magic   97

11 Engaging Conflict: Learning to Balance Power   106

12 Forgiveness: Choosing How You Want to Live   116

13 The Art of Reconciliation: Imagining a Just Future 128

PART IV
Just Musings   141

Index   *144*

ACKNOWLEDGMENTS

Over a decade ago I was encouraged to teach a course that involved service learning. I had a desire to help disadvantaged groups, but didn't really know how to go about it, so I called my friend Kit Danley, President of Neighborhood Ministries. We worked together to construct an experience for students that would involve hands-on practice with low-income, urban populations, and exposure to writings about generational poverty. Let me reiterate, I knew almost nothing about what I was doing. Thank you, Kit, for walking by my side as I have taught this class every semester for over ten years. Equally, I want to thank my students who have written journals, created presentations, written papers, and come into my office lit up with joy! Thank you for teaching me what it means to work with people who are different from yourself. And, special thanks to Shanae G. for opening your heart and sharing your poetry with me. Thank you to my guest speakers. As I listened to you all, I kept finding links between what you were talking about and what I was teaching in my other classes. It is largely because of you that I have written this book. Also, thanks (and possibly apologies!) to my friends whose stories show up in various ways in this book. You've always known it was dangerous to let me know very much about your lives.

A special thanks to Janie Bryant, who did a tremendous amount of work collecting material for this book, and who read early versions of many chapters—we don't always see eye to eye on things, but that is often what I have needed. May you listen to the muses on your own journey. I also want to specifically acknowledge Kathleen Galvin and James Baesler for their many wonderful insights—this is definitely a stronger, more cohesive book because of you. Thanks to all of you who looked at early versions of these chapters, Nicki Piemonte (who graciously saved me from using certain archaic phrases in the case studies—your edits were totes cray!),

Jay Taylor, students in my courses Inner-City Families and Relational Communication, and my wife, Ann, who is an editor *extraordinaire*!

Finally, thank you to Mitch Allen at Left Coast Press who originally had the foresight to pick up this project, and the fortitude to take the risk. And, also, to Linda, Stephanie, and the staff at Routledge—thank you so much for welcoming me into your family of authors, putting me at ease, being open to change, and making me feel at home.

Doug
Phoenix, AZ
June 25, 2016

FOREWORD

When I hear the word "justice," like many people I think immediately of *social* justice, of the state where all people get to live in the full embodiment of their rights. I also think of the efforts *toward* social justice—the myriad people and groups who work tirelessly to create conditions in which those without true social justice may experience more of it than they have had. Before reading *Just Relationships*, I had seldom thought about justice at the personal and relational level. Now, I can see clearly that justice—or attempts at such justice—exists all around us. Now, I think of our relationships as places where people can and should be able to live out their full humanity, as they support their relational partners' rights to the same. I am grateful for this shift in worldview.

In *Just Relationships*, Dr. Kelley reveals a way to think about relationships that is truly game-changing. Most books on interpersonal relationships are either descriptive accounts of academic work that help reflect the complexity of what it means to be connected to one another, or they take a nonresearch-based stance offering a means for thinking about our relationships in new ways, ways that may or may not be consistent with what scholars know about the intricacies of communication and relating. In this book, Dr. Kelley provides a "new way," but he uses existing research to do so. Additionally, the "new way" provides a means for understanding those research findings in a larger, richer context.

Many of the processes brought forward in this book are things with which interpersonal and relational scholars are familiar. Conflict, trust, and persuasive communication are part of many texts. But in *Just Relationships*, Dr. Kelley gracefully builds a narrative into which these processes arise organically rather than as a set of topics relevant to a given area of study, but otherwise acontextual. For example, we often talk about facework processes as activities in which people engage in their interactions with others. But in this book, facework is seen within the context of working to be ourselves in relationship to others and as a means to allow others to also live out their full selves. As such, the process of facework becomes more than just an interesting set of observations. We can see that it can both aid us in our attempts at personal and relational justice when others work with us to ensure our positive face, and serve as a way to enact facades that, even if we come out "looking good," are actually moments of inauthenticity. As such, looking at relational and communicative processes, such as facework, through a justice lens allows us to see those processes in new ways.

The concept of morality is, on the other hand, one that most relationship and communication researchers seldom use. Indeed when Dr. Kelley and his colleague Vince Waldron asked me to be on a conference panel about morality in relationships and to contribute to their book, *Moral Talk Across the Lifespan*, I did not think, as a "secular" scholar, that I had anything to offer. But I joined in anyway, and through it—and this book—I have been able to understand that we do—as researchers and as people (secular and otherwise)—think in terms of good/bad and right/wrong in our interactions with others. In *Just Relationships*, Dr. Kelley shows further what this means and why it is an important framework to understand how we exist in our relationships and make choices in our communication with others. That is, when we think of ourselves and others in terms of our humanity and the best ways to be in relationship with others, we see relationship and communicative constructs in a very different light. It further and more fully helps us to understand the processes that we teach and that we live.

But this sense of a moral (i.e., equitable, growth-based, fair, self-efficacious) way to be does not prescribe a set of behaviors separate from the complexity of living. For instance, Dr. Kelley urges us to be advocates, to rehumanize others when we feel hurt by them, to have open dialogue. At the same time, he also talks about the very real human conditions that make this process difficult. He shows us work that reveals that, as emotional and cognitive beings, there are forces that encourage us to stay unchanged or to leave rather than to engage. Thus, Dr. Kelley offers us a path but does not hide the fact that the way is littered with roots that may trip us up and forks that may take us in a different direction. The "story" he provides is one that presents relationships as a place where we can be bettered if we think in terms of justice—living in our full humanity and valuing the same for our relational partners. This book enlivens our understanding of the complexities and promises of pursuing relationships in this way.

But there's more. *Just Relationships* not only increases our understanding of the everyday processes in which we engage—and the inherent struggles we may face when we do so—it also gives us ample opportunity to see these processes in action. Through his *Living It Out* questions, we are provided a chance to contemplate our own worldviews, beliefs, and values and the "mythologies" that we accept as truth. And through the case studies—many drawn from real life experiences—we get a glimpse into how the processes can take particular form. Dr. Kelley also shares examples from his own life, showing how even a relational communication "expert" confronts challenges to what he teaches and studies. His candor humanizes even further the concepts that he encourages us to understand.

Finally, Dr. Kelley provides ideas from a broad range of origins. He uses research not just from interpersonal and relational communication scholars, he reveals the relevance of scholarship in other traditions. For example, Dr. Kelley applies Patrice Buzzanell's work on organizational resilience as an ideal way to think about what people build within themselves and within interpersonal relationships. He also brings in ideas from "popular" sources, such as Brene Brown's important work on shame and vulnerability and Marshall Rosenberg's concept of Nonviolent Communication, both of which have at their base *respect for self and other*. In doing so he shows that justice and injustice permeate the way we move through all aspects of our lives.

As teachers and learners we benefit from the breadth of ideas that *Just Relationships* provides. As a communication scholar, I also value the central premise that engaging in just relationships is fully a *communicative practice*, negotiated and experienced in everyday moments and across the cycle of our relationships and our lives.

Valerie Manusov

PREFACE

The Just Path

Just Relationships is designed to help teachers, students, practitioners, researchers, and relational partners engage in genuine dialogue about how we, together, can create relationships that are just. The essence of justice is creating spaces where relationship partners are able to embrace their full humanity, that is, where each of us can fully become . . . us. In this vein, *Just Relationships* reexamines social scientific theory and research to better understand how to create positive, vibrant, healthy personal relationships.

Just Relationships is written in a manner to encourage good thinking about important social justice topics (e.g., advocacy, dehumanization, love, shame, forgiveness, and reconciliation), within dyadic communication contexts. As such, the focus of the book is how we relate, *justly*, to our *relationship partners*—that is, anyone with whom you are in a relationship, including children, friends, parents, and lovers. To this end, each chapter begins with an overview of a particular conceptual realm (e.g., equity, attributions, forgiveness). For instance, in Chapter Two: "Just Relationships" I discuss how equity, equality, and need are related to notions of justice. This brief overview of research and theory focuses on possible implications and questions related to how our interpersonal relationships are the most basic places where we practice justice.

Building on this foundation of theory linked to practice, a hallmark of *Just Relationships* is learning through application. The second half of each chapter is focused on specific application of the concepts and theories previously covered, including a section I call *Living It Out*. *Living It Out* offers specific suggestions to apply *justice* concepts to interpersonal relationships. In addition, each chapter ends with two case studies and questions to encourage deeper thinking about the cases. These cases are designed to remind us of the broad spectrum of relationships that need to be lived justly. Some of the cases are true stories, but don't get stuck on the specific examples—feel free to alter cases in terms of gender, age, race, ethnicity, socioeconomic status, or any other characteristic that will make the case more meaningful to you.

The book is structured in three parts. *Part I: Imagining Just Relationships: Perspectives* provides a conceptual framework for understanding social justice within an interpersonal context. Here I argue that just relationships are relationships wherein we are free to pursue our full humanity. They are moral and equitable partnerships, characterized by some type of appropriate connection consisting of trust and respect, and co-created space where each individual finds their own voice. In this first section, Chapter Two: "Just Relationships" examines relational partners' experience of justice in relationships, especially as it relates to notions of equity, fairness, and respect, and emphasizes justice as process. Chapter Three: "Good Relationships" conceptualizes personal relationships as moral entities, strongly suggesting that genuine dialogue creates a space for individuals to become more fully human, and that *justice is really about the freedom to pursue our own humanity.* Chapter Four: "Love Relationships" focuses on ideas of connection, specifically intimacy, commitment, emotional bonding, and other-centeredness, and argues that love is the only tenable way of pursuing long-term justice in our personal relationships. Chapter Five: "Interpersonal Advocacy: Creating Spaces" conceptualizes interpersonal advocacy as love in action, and develops the notion that through *creating spaces where if something good can happen, it will,* individuals are enabled to find and speak their own voice.

Part II: Barriers to Just Relationships: Perceptions That Separate explores a number of familiar interpersonal concepts that have applied social justice implications as they potentially limit our pursuit of social justice. This section begins by examining perception and its effect on how we see others and ourselves and, subsequently, focuses on how we often limit our pursuit of justice in our thoughts and actions. Chapter Six: "Worldview: Your Relationship Frame" examines how our relationship frames (relationship worldviews) influence our perception of relationships and, as such, influence how we respond to relationship partners. Chapter Seven: "Dehumanizing the 'Other'" extends the previous chapter with a focus on processes that often exclude and dehumanize others in our lives. Chapter Eight: "Saving Face" looks at how personal identity and facework shape responses to others, especially during conflict episodes, and can inhibit our pursuit of just relationships if we aren't aware of them. Chapter Nine: "Shame on You, Shame on Me" makes clear distinctions between shame and guilt, suggesting that shame often works against the relational goals we desire, and offers suggestions for productive ways to take responsibility for one's actions.

Part III: Shaping Just Relationships: Creating a Just Future looks at interpersonal processes that create space for negotiating and building just relationships. Chapter Ten: "Resilience: Ordinary Magic" highlights personal and relational characteristics that help individuals and relationships avoid personal and relational pitfalls and bounce back after difficulty. Chapter Eleven: "Engaging Conflict" examines constructive conflict principles, emphasizing that a balance of power is essential to achieving justice. Chapter Twelve: "Forgiveness: Choosing How You Want to Live" focuses on forgiveness as one means of healing the past in order to move toward a just future. Chapter Thirteen: "The Art of Reconciliation: Imagining a Just Future" pulls the previous chapters together by emphasizing emotional healing as the means to developing trust and commitment, and offering imagination as a method to bring people together. The book finishes with a section called *Just Musings*. As the title suggests, here I look back over the book and pull the strands and threads together. This section ends with a simple poem, "I," that sums up the essence of this project.

Using This Book

Just Relationships is designed to be used in college classrooms, for training of practitioners, and for individual growth and reflection. For the college classroom, most of the theories covered will be familiar to social science scholars. As such, it makes a good supplement to help instructors and students deal with the questions that most of us are already asking ourselves, and that naturally come up in relationship-based courses. Although there is a progression of thought inherent in the chapter progression (I develop this in Chapter One: "Just Thoughts"), chapters can be used out of order. In one of my courses, Inner-City Families, we start with the first chapter and work our way straight through to the last. However, when I use the book in my Relational Communication course, I use the chapters out of order, based more on what theories are covered rather than the sequential chapter development in the book.

For practitioners, *Just Relationships* provides a theoretical perspective for what many of you are already doing. However, in today's world where our workforce and volunteers are highly educated, this book provides a way to think about what may seem rather *natural* to you. In this since, *Just Relationships* may offer new perspective or remind you of what you already believe. It is also a good resource to train new staff and volunteers, many of whom have good hearts and desires, but little training to help them think through the oft-unsettling process of advocating for and with others.

Those of you who have picked up this book for personal growth and reflection, I strongly suggest that you keep a journal as you read through *Just Relationships*. Write openly about what ideas are challenging you, resonating with you, or difficult for you to hold on to. Make it personal by reading each section with a person, or persons, in mind.

In whatever way you have found yourself holding *Just Relationships,* I hope you will take time to savor the pages ahead. Don't rush through them. Let the ideas work their way into your imagination. Take time to learn through *Living It Out,* avoiding the fallacy that "real learning" is only in your head. Let this book work its way into the fabric of your life.

CASES AND CONCEPTS

PART I
Imagining Just Relationships: Perspectives   **1**

2 Just Relationships   9
    Concepts—Distributive Justice (Equity, Equality, Need),
    Processual Justice (e.g., Respect), Nonviolence
    2.1 Regina Feels Her Seven-Year Marriage to Gustavo
        Is out of Balance   16
    2.2 Guicho, a Former Gang Member, Learns Justice from
        a Youth He Is Working With   17

3 Good Relationships   19
    Concepts—Morality, *Negotiated Morality Theory*, Dialogue
    (Genuine Dialogue, Dialogue Principles and Acts), Mindfulness
    3.1 Long-Time Friends, John and Sameer, Argue over a
        Dating Situation Where Sameer Feels Betrayed   26
    3.2 LaShanna Is Frustrated and Confused as She Tries to Mentor
        Debbie, a 19-Year-Old Single Mom   27

4 Love Relationships   30
    Concepts—Full Love, Commitment, Emotional Bonding,
    Other-Centeredness (Self-Sacrifice), Ubuntu,
    Vulnerability, Intimacy
    4.1 Joanna and Kermit Are Dating, and Joanna Thinks
        She Is "in Love"   36
    4.2 As Parents, Ashley and James Have to Deal with
        Rebecca's Difficult Behavior   37

5 Interpersonal Advocacy: Creating Spaces   40
     Concepts—Advocacy Approaches, Mentoring, Mutuality,
     Mindfulness, Peer Support, Play
     5.1 Brenda Becomes an Advocate for Her Son, Tyler,
           When He Loses His Job   48
     5.2 Cynthia Is Frustrated in Her Mentoring Relationship
           with Paige and Quits   50

PART II
Barriers to Just Relationships: Perceptions That Separate   53

6 Worldview: Your Relationship Frame   55
     Concepts—Worldview, Relationship Framing, Dominance-
     Submissiveness (Control-Submission) and Affiliation-
     Disaffiliation (Connection-Distance), Attributions
     (Relationship-Enhancing, Distress-Maintaining),
     Relationship Myths, Attachment, Framing (Early) Recollections
     6.1 Katie's Struggle to Handle Her Breakup with Matt Highlights
           Some Unhealthy Ways That She Sees Herself and Others   64
     6.2 When Martin Is Arrested for Stealing a Car, Ramon
           (His Mentor) Realizes the Differences in How They
           See Themselves and the World in Which They Live   65

7 Dehumanizing the "Other"   67
     Concepts—Dehumanization, Infrahumanization,
     Emotion, Ethnocentrism, Imagination
     7.1 Sabrina Is Put in Difficult Position When Her Mom
           Confides in Her after Her Mom and Dad's Divorce   74
     7.2 Victor and Luis Are Former Gang Members Who
           Eventually Work Together   74

8 Saving Face   76
     Concepts—Face, Facework (Building and Protecting),
     Goals of Interaction, Conflict, Dialogue, Abuse
     8.1 Kat and Lydia's Face Issues Are Making Conversations Difficult   82
     8.2 John Has Become Aggressive in His Relationship with
           Carrie, but He Is Defensive When She Tries to Discuss
           the Issue with Him   83

9 Shame on You, Shame on Me   85
     Concepts—Shame, Guilt, Blame, Attribution
     (Relationship-Enhancing, Distress-Maintaining,
     Defensiveness, Responsibility, Shame Resilience

9.1 Barrett and Jamie Have Sex, and Jamie Is Now Pregnant.
Through Counsel with a Mentor They Decide to Tell Their Parents   92
9.2 As a First-Generation College Student, Jessica Is Trying
to Believe in Herself, While Her Boyfriend, Carlos,
Feels Threatened by Her Success   93

PART III
Shaping Just Relationships: Creating a Just Future   95

10 Resilience: Ordinary Magic   97
Concepts—Resilience (Preventive and Promotive Factors),
Risk, Adaptability, Change
10.1 Nicole Contacts Her Friend Carmen to Help Her Think
through Her Decision to Move to California   103
10.2 As a New Teacher in an Urban School, Sandra
Tries to Understand Terri's Family Situation and Help
Her Succeed Academically   104

11 Engaging Conflict: Learning to Balance Power   106
Concepts—Homeostasis, Resistance to Change, Mindlessness,
Arousal, Mindfulness, Relationship Messages, Power, Power
Balancing, Transcendent Discourse
11.1 Courtney and Belinda Have Conflict as They Plan Their
Mother's Memorial Service   113
11.2 Sam and His Dad Are Having Conflict over Whether He
Can Quit the College Baseball Team   114

12 Forgiveness: Choosing How You Want to Live   116
Concepts—Forgiveness, Hurt, Mercy, Emotions (Hard and Soft),
Voice, Empathy, Renegotiation, Truth, Understanding
12.1 Carlos Considers Forgiving Lidia after She Kisses
Someone at Work   124
12.2 When Stacie Is Forced to Take Care of Her Aging Mother,
She Works through Forgiving Her for Not Being the Mother
She Always Wished She Would Be   125

13 The Art of Reconciliation: Imagining a Just Future   128
Concepts—Reconciliation, Trust, Commitment, Emotional
Healing, Apology, Imagining the Future, Boundaries
13.1 Ty's Dad Struggles with Ty's Search for Sexual Identity   136
13.2 Lori's Absent Father Contacts Her after Years of Being Absent   137

PART I

Imagining Just Relationships

Perspectives

1

JUST THOUGHTS

Most people sense whether their relationships are fair or not. "Do I put in more effort?" "Do I always initiate?" "Have I been hurt more deeply?" "Am I respected?" "Do I have equal opportunities to grow as a person? To do what I like? To be happy? To just be me?!"

Relationships are moral entities (Austin & Tobiasen, 1982; Kelley, 2012b; Waldron & Kelley, 2008). People view many relational behaviors and events from a moral framework. That is, they often interpret actions within relationships as right or wrong, good or bad. Relationship partners have a seemingly innate sense as to fairness or appropriateness in their relationships. Individuals, especially in Western cultures, also gauge whether their relationship partners are restricting them from growth or personal expression. In these ways, social relationships are evaluated in terms of whether they are *just* relationships, especially when things seem out of balance ("I'm pulling all the weight in this relationship," "How could you do that to me?" "Wait a minute, I have a say in this, too!").

Social justice has been a term predominately used to discuss disadvantaged persons. Disadvantaged typically refers to a lack of equality between groups or individuals. For example, equity disparity between the sexes or between racial or cultural groups has been a much studied and referenced social justice issue (Frey, 2009). Inevitably, social justice inequities are rooted in power disadvantages—typically, one group, compared to the other, has more of a sense of self-efficacy. That is, they have greater opportunity to influence their own lives.

Self-efficacy, the ability to influence one's own life (Bandura, 1997), results from access to resources (e.g., finances, status, skill sets, and even nurturing), knowledge and ability to execute certain social behaviors (e.g., argumentation), and the ability to achieve desired goals (e.g., a proven track record of achievement, and availability of opportunities). Unequal distribution of these elements between groups or individuals may be viewed as unjust, unfair, and, often, as morally wrong. Injustice may also be evident when procedures to 'right' these 'wrongs' are not equally applied to all parties involved. For example, one of the functions of a judge is to ensure plaintiff and defendant adhere to the same protocol during courtroom proceedings. As such, social justice themes often focus on equity, equality, fairness, power imbalance, empowerment, identity, resources, and morality.

These themes are represented throughout research on interpersonal relationships, although common terminology often mitigates seeing interpersonal relationships in light of a moral or justice lens (e.g., terms such as *extradyadic relationship* and *extradyadic sex* are used by certain writers to remove the value-orientation of words such as *infidelity* and *adultery*; Allan & Harrison, 2009). Traditional social science–based theories that focus on equity, power, attachment, attribution, conflict, identity, and forgiveness and reconciliation are, essentially, embedded in what relational partners often see as moral, or value-laden, contexts. As such, these theories (e.g., equity theory, attribution theory) can be used to better understand partners' responses to perceived inequity or transgression.

Certain researchers have specifically written about justice in interpersonal contexts (De Cremer, van Kleef, & Wubben, 2007; Lamm, 1986). My own writing on forgiveness (2012b) suggests that one reason people are motivated to forgive is to restore the moral order of the relationship. Other forgiveness researchers have focused on the justice gap (Exline, Worthington, Hill, & McCullough, 2003) or the perception of certain transgressions, such as infidelity, as moral wrongs (Kelley, 2012a).

The goal of *Just Relationships* is to examine interpersonal relationships through a social justice lens. Here I use existing social science theory in an effort to frame interpersonal relationships from a social justice perspective. A few early social psychology works focused on justice in interpersonal relationships (Bierhoff, Cohen, & Greenberg, 1986; Greenberg & Cohen, 1982), as does a current research program by Mel Lerner and colleagues, who believe that "psychologists [all social scientists] can and should conduct research on issues of critical social significance" (Ross & Miller, 2002). Yet, focusing on interpersonal relationships as moral entities (e.g., relationship partners construct relationship ethics that guide the determination of "right" and "wrong" behavior) has not been a common perspective in social science research. Recently, during a meeting with a local, practicing psychologist, I mentioned that I was working on a proposal for a book that would look at interpersonal relationships using social justice language. Her eyes brightened. "That would be fascinating!" As nice as it was to hear, it concerned me that this person hadn't taken time think about relationships from a justice, or moral, framework. Likewise, a few years ago, Vince Waldron and I hosted an event at our national conference, focusing on how morality emerges and is expressed in interpersonal relationships. Many of the scholars who participated, all of whom were nationally recognized researchers, expressed appreciation for being challenged to think about their own work in moral terms. Most of them had never made this conceptual move.

A Social Justice Framework for Interpersonal Relationships

There is a significant flow of thought to the chapters of this book. Let me take a moment to give you a brief framework to help you follow my thinking. *Just Relationships* is designed to look at aspects of relationships often overlooked by social scientists, but often most important to relational partners. For instance, in my research with couples married 30–80 years (Waldron & Kelley, 2008), many marriage partners talked about respect as the most important element of making their relationships last. Others highlighted the importance of balance, equality, fairness, and unselfishness (Kelley, 2015). These concepts represent moral aspects of these couples' relationships. From their perspective, they are ways that you "should" be with one another. In addition, *Just Relationships* takes research, set in traditional social justice settings (e.g., see Chapter Seven: "Dehumanizing the 'Other'"), and applies it to our personal relationships. With all of these elements in mind, the following chapters lay out key concepts to imagine and shape our personal relationships in a just manner.

Just Relationships begins with *Part I: Imagining Just Relationships: Perspectives* where together we explore conceptual foundations for the rest of the book. Here we look at the nature of justice, with a focus on justice as process. Then we move on to explore justice as part of the moral ethic each of us develops within each of our relationships, and emphasize dialogue as more than a means of negotiating morality, but also a means of experiencing morality itself. Importantly, justice and morality are seen as spaces in which individuals can experience their full humanity. Keeping this in mind, we venture into unexpected territory by exploring love as the most efficient means of achieving justice in long-term relationships. Not sentimental love, but love based on commitment, deep emotional bonds, and other-centeredness. Finally, advocacy is offered as a means of understanding love in action, and interpersonal advocacy is conceptualized as bringing hope through *creating a space where if something good can happen, it will.*

The four foundational chapters set a tone that is practical, but also somewhat idyllic. Thus, we have to ask, *All of this sounds good, so why aren't our relationships just? Part II: Barriers to Just Relationships: Perceptions That Separate* examines four phenomena that help explain why we often fail to live justly. We begin by looking at how our worldviews, or relational frames as I call them, often restrict our ability to see others and understand their experience. This often leads to the creation of ingroup and outgroup experiences that culminate in dehumanization. So, our restricted relational frames and tendency to dehumanize those who are different from us work against treating others justly. In addition to dehumanizing others in our lives, we tend to get sidetracked from justice by protecting our own identity and public face. And, somewhat counterintuitively, we find that when we experience our own shame it often draws us away from others and undermines our ability to imagine and shape just relationships.

Assuming we can manage some of the barriers to living justly, how do we begin to shape relationships that are characterized by justice? *Part III: Shaping Just Relationships: Creating a Just Future* looks at four processes essential to redeeming our broken relationships and broken selves. We begin by looking at resilience, examining notions of risk, protective factors, and characteristics associated with the ability to positively adapt and change. This is followed by a focus on conflict practices, specifically looking at how to manage mindless behavior and high arousal in order to restore a balance of power to broken relationships. But, power balance is difficult to achieve without emotional healing through forgiveness, so we go there next—recognizing that apart from emotional healing, it is extremely difficult for relational partners to work through their differences in a humane manner. Finally, reconciliation. Here we examine the development, or reestablishment, of trust and commitment with appropriate boundaries, so that relational partners have a safe space to rebuild their relationship.

The final portion, *Part IV: Just Musings*, reflects on the process of writing this book, and reminds you of where we've been, and where we might be going. The closing poem, "I," gives you something to ponder as you leaf back through the book reflecting on your own *just* journey.

A Personal Note

My experience has been that people who do not hold a healthy understanding of relationship justice stay stuck in never-ending loops of anger, hurt, frustration, and hopelessness. I have written this book to help us think more broadly and deeply about justice in our relationships and, as such, to help us all get unstuck from unproductive patterns that work against our connecting and respecting.

My counseling degree has taught me that most people only come for help when they feel stuck. My forgiveness research with couples has taught me that people need help working through, or living with, hurt—otherwise they stay stuck in cycles of extreme emotion and confused sense-making. My connection to inner-city organizations has taught me how people often stay stuck in the cycle of poverty if they don't have someone to help them see hope in a new perspective. In each of these settings, a myopic view of justice (i.e., a limited view of what is fair or "right" in a relationship) can blind individuals as to how to move forward in their lives.

To this point, ten years ago I began teaching a course at Arizona State University entitled Inner-City Families. I didn't know much about inner-city families at the time, I simply thought it was important that students be exposed to people who live near them but don't have the same opportunities that they have. I offer the course every semester and it is repeatable for credit so that a student working with a 10-year-old, poor, urban student in the fall can stay with him or her for an entire year, continuing to get credit in the spring. I have students read academic material about low-income, urban populations, and I bring in guest speakers who do "real" work in the city. But all of this is simply to get students to reflect on the three hours of service a week that they volunteer as part of the course. In her final paper this year, one of my students, Debbie, wrote of her own experience in life, and in the class:

> An important concept I learned was how the poverty cycle works. When Kit Danley came to our class to speak about the poverty cycle, I was truly amazed. I could relate to immigration, jobs, and education because my current partner is an immigrant and we are going through the poverty cycle right now. I am educating myself for a better future, but education is not all it takes for you to get out of the cycle. Having my partner as an illegal immigrant keeps us from getting out of the cycle because he is so limited in this country. . . . All of this brings his self-esteem down, and he feels shame about who he is and what he does, which almost obligates him to get back into the poverty cycle. I now know it is up to me whether to stay in the cycle of poverty or do something about it. Today, I am doing something to change my life. Life is not easy, but neither is it impossible.

My dream for this book is that important interpersonal relationship scholarship can be used to create more loving and just personal relationships by helping all kinds of people, in all kinds of relationships, get unstuck—that, like Debbie, someday you will be able to say, I used this book to "change my life" and the lives of those I love.

References

Allan, G., & Harrison, K. (2009). Affairs and infidelity. In A. Vangelisti (Ed.), *Feeling hurt in close relationships* (pp. 191–208). New York: Cambridge University Press.

Austin, W., & Tobiasen, J. (1982). Moral evaluation in intimate relationships. In J. Greenberg & R. L. Cohen (Eds.), *Equity and justice in social behavior* (pp. 217–259). New York: Academic Press.

Bandura, A. (1997). *Self-efficacy: The exercise of control.* New York: Henry Holt & Co.

Bierhoff, H. W., Cohen, R. L., & Greenberg, J. (1986). *Justice in social relations.* New York: Plenum.

De Cremer, D., van Kleef, G. A., & Wubben, M. J. J. (2007). Do the emotions of others shape justice effects?: An interpersonal approach. In D. De Cremer (Ed.), *Advances in the psychology of justice and affect* (pp. 37–59). Charlotte, NC: Information Age Publishing.

Exline, J. J., Worthington, E. L., Hill, P., & McCullough, M. E. (2003). Forgiveness and justice: A research agenda for social and personality psychology. *Personality and Social Psychology Review, 7,* 337–348.

Frey, L. R. (2009). Social justice. In S. W. Littlejohn & K. A. Foss (Eds.), *Encyclopedia of communication theory* (Vol. 2, pp. 908–911). Thousand Oaks, CA: Sage.

Greenberg, J., & Cohen, R. L. (1982). *Equity and justice in social behavior.* New York: Academic Press.

Kelley, D. L. (2012a). *Marital communication*. Cambridge, UK: Polity.

Kelley, D. L. (2012b). Forgiveness as restoration: The search for well-being, reconciliation, and relational justice. In T. J. Socha & M. J. Pitts (Eds.), *The positive side of interpersonal communication* (pp. 193–210). New York: Peter Lang.

Kelley, D. L. (2015). Just marriage. In V. Waldron & D. Kelley (Eds.), *Moral talk across the lifespan: Creating good relationships* (pp. 75–94). New York: Peter Lang.

Lamm, H. (1986). Justice considerations in interpersonal conflict. In H. W. Bierhoff, R. L. Cohen, & J. Greenberg (Eds.), *Justice in social relations* (pp. 43–63). New York: Plenum Press.

Ross, M., & Miller, D. T. (2002). Overview of the volume. In M. Ross & D. T. Miller (Eds.), *The justice motive in everyday life* (pp. 3–9). Cambridge: Cambridge University Press.

Waldron, V. R., & Kelley, D. L. (2008). *Communicating forgiveness*. Thousand Oaks, CA: Sage.

2

JUST RELATIONSHIPS

Relational partners have a seemingly innate sense of whether or not things are "just." "I'm always the one to clean the kitchen." "You never initiate." "When you borrow my truck you don't refill it with gas." "You hurt me, and 'I'm sorry' is supposed to make everything okay?" "Is there some way I can make things up to you?" or "Hey, you owe me big time for what happened!"

Social justice is often associated with notions of equity and equality. At this writing, the United States believes that North Korea is responsible for a cyber attack against Sony Pictures. In his retort, President Obama has stated, "We will respond proportionately" (USA Today, 2014). President Obama's statement equates a just response with a proportionate response. The hope is to restore balance by responding in an equitable manner.

Relational justice is a form of social justice that we experience or desire in our interpersonal relationships. As the opening examples demonstrate, it is often illustrated as, "That's not fair!" The common parental phrase, "Life isn't fair," could be restated as, "You don't always experience justice in this life" or "Things, simply, are not equal for everyone." Sometimes, there are two of you and 13 M&Ms, and someone is going to get 7, and it's just not fair. However, social justice is much more complicated than that, and relational justice is often experienced in many other nonequity manifestations. At the core of social and relational justice is the right and ability for each of us to grow into our fullness as human beings. Put another way, just relationships are safe spaces where each of us is free to become our whole self. That stated, we begin our discussion by looking at a few key concepts related to how we often think of and experience justice in our interpersonal relationships.

The Justice Motive

When individuals use phrases like, "Life isn't fair," it is because as children we all develop a *justice motive* (Lerner, 1980, 2002). Through careful observation of human behavior, children conclude that certain actions typically result in certain general outcomes. When this perceived pattern has been reified, or set firmly in one's mind, a justice ethic has emerged. Outcomes that are consistent with one's justice ethic are perceived as "good" or "right," and outcomes that are dissonant with one's justice expectations are perceived as "bad" or "wrong." As such, when one's experience matches what one thinks "should" happen, it is concluded that justice has occurred. Put in popular terms—justice is getting what you deserve.

Four Ways to Think about Relational Justice

Getting what one deserves suggests we should be treated in a certain manner (e.g., with respect) and that various elements in relationships should be fairly distributed. Let's begin with distribution. Relational partners expect fair distribution of resources, outcomes (both positive and negative), and effort. Morton Deutsch (2006, 2011) suggests guiding principles for distribution of these relationship elements (often referred to as distributive justice): *equity*, *equality*, and *need* represent the first three ways to think about justice.

Equity represents people's desire for rewards commensurate with the effort they've expended. In other words, the biggest investors should get the biggest return on their effort or risk. I don't mind if you get more out, if you put more in. Central to this idea is that not everyone values the same *relationship currencies*. A currency is something that is used for exchange of resources within a particular relationship or community. In personal relationships, currencies can be anything from respect to affection to understanding. For example, a young couple that works hard all day has to negotiate their end-of-the-day rewards. Because he is socially oriented, it sounds relaxing to him that, together, they debrief their day over a couple glasses of wine; for her, relaxation comes by shutting down in a long, hot bath. For him, talking is a valuable currency used to unwind after a hard day; for her, silence is golden. Likewise, a mentor for a young urban teen might see the time she gives to their relationship as a valuable currency, whereas the teen may not value that time in the early stages of their relationship.

Equality, when related to fair distribution, suggests relational partners share equivalent rewards and costs in the relationship. Deutsch (2006, 2011) proposes that this perspective on distribution might be most prevalent when individuals are focused on relational themes such as closeness and cohesiveness. Although relational partners value different currencies, they may want certain elements of the relationship to be experienced equally. For example, my own research with married couples has demonstrated that loving one another equally is important to partners (Kelley, 2015). On the flip side, when hurt, relational partners often struggle with the idea of forgiveness because it feels unfair that partners have not experienced pain equally. In this sense, revenge can be an attempt to achieve justice by equaling the pain, hurt, or negative consequences experienced by each partner. (I discuss this in more detail in Chapter 12: "Forgiveness.")

The third principle guiding relational distribution is need. *Need* is a critical aspect to experiencing justice in lasting, committed relationships. This is perhaps most easily seen in a parent's relationship with her rebellious daughter. There is little equity in the relationship—Mom gets sparse appreciation for driving her 15-year-old daughter to various events. And, often, little equality—Mom tells her daughter she would like to spend time with her and the daughter responds, "Why would I want to spend time with you when I don't even like you?!" However, Mom may not experience this situation as unfair. Though she may experience various emotions such as hurt, pain, and fear, she may also be guided by the need principle—"My daughter has the greater need at this point. She is struggling for autonomy and to find her own 'adult' identity." Because she wants to help her daughter make the difficult transition into adulthood, she is willing to put in more than her share of the effort in the relationship. Thus, although the relationship is not equitable or equal in many ways, Mom may perceive it to be fair—"After all," she thinks, "I am the adult." As you might guess, the need principle is often most prominent in situations where need is exacerbated by undue stress, such as disability, illness, financial crises, family issues, developmental struggles, and career- or school-related issues.

At the beginning of this section I framed our discussion in light of the popular perspective that justice is *getting what you deserve*. Thus far we've discussed understanding getting what you deserve in light of equity, equality, and need. But, getting what you deserve can also mean that we all *deserve* to be treated in a just manner. As such, the fourth way to think about justice is process. Rather than focusing on the *equity-*, *equality-*, or *need-*based distribution of resources, effort, and consequences in one's relationships, *processual justice* focuses on the processes in the relationship itself. For example, do relational partners think they are generally treated in a fair manner? (Similarly, previous researchers have discussed procedural justice, a term that seems too administrative to describe personal relationships. Therefore, I've used the phrase "processual justice" to focus on all aspects of process in personal relationships; see Kelley, 2015). Being treated fairly includes the establishment of fair relationship rules, fair interaction qualities, and the overall perception that the relationship is a fair one. Establishing fair relationship rules includes the emergence of informal norms (e.g., everyone gets an opportunity to voice their opinions) or the creation of more formal policies and rules (e.g., when mediating between siblings, a parent may lay out explicit guidelines—"No name calling while we discuss what happened."). In addition, being treated fairly typically includes certain interaction qualities (e.g., being spoken to with respect). Interacting respectfully includes such elements as listening to understand and treating others' ideas as valid, even if you disagree with them. Finally, when process elements are viewed as fair and respectful, partners have a general sense that they are in a *just relationship*. That is, I believe my partner is doing her best to treat me fairly, with respect. Creating just process is very much what Marshall Rosenberg's 2015 bestseller,

TABLE 2.1 Words Indicating Justice in Long-term Marriages

Distributive	*Processual*
Fair	Balance
Fifty-fifty	Honesty
Unselfish	Civility
Jealousy	Commitment
More	True/untrue
Respect	Respect
Equality	Equality
Accommodation	Agreement
Understanding	

Nonviolent Communication, is all about. Responding nonviolently is life enhancing and, as I highlight at the beginning of this chapter, that means it moves us toward growth and embraces our full humanity (more about this later).

Recently I examined transcripts from couples married 30–80 years (yes, 80!) for words that demonstrate some sense of justice ethic in their marriages (Kelley, 2015). What I found was that, indeed, partners' statements reflected both the distributive and processual aspects of justice. Couples used words like fair, fifty-fifty, unselfish, jealousy, more, respect, equality, and accommodation to address how resources or effort were distributed in the relationship. Processual words included equal, respect, balance, honesty, civility, commitment, true/untrue, agreement, and understood, and seemed to indicate expectations that partners would act in a fair manner with one another.

A final word about believing that your relationship is, essentially, just. Believing our relationship is just stabilizes the relationship as we operate in an imperfect world where our individual interactions are not always fair. A justice-oriented relationship worldview (which I further develop in Chapter Six: "Worldview") serves as a heuristic, a guide to decision making, that streamlines the process of evaluating justice issues in the relationship (Lind, 2001). That is, as adults we recognize that "perfect justice" can seldom be achieved when regarding complex issues. However, if we believe a particular relationship to be just (a component of processual justice), then in any given circumstance we may choose to trust that our partner has made the best decision possible given the circumstances, and has taken into account both of our needs and desires. In this way, we may evaluate a specific decision as just even though it is not perfectly "fair" in the moment.

Building Just Relationships

Relational partners build just relationships by negotiating their own relationship justice ethic. That is, relationship partners either implicitly or explicitly *co-create* what they consider *fair* in the relationship. This ethic must take into account how resources, outcomes (both positive and negative), and effort are distributed in the relationship. In addition, the partners must come to a mutual understanding of fair process—that is, how they are to treat one another in a *just* manner.

Preparing for Justice: Determine "What Counts as What"

Understanding what is important to one another creates a sound foundation as relational partners negotiate what is fair in their relationship. Individuals can begin the justice process by seeking to understand what is of value to each person. For example, a parent would be wise to check out her perceptions as to what is valued by her daughter before trying to motivate her using the equity principle—the promise of shopping together after completing household chores will only seem like an equitable reward if the daughter values time shopping with Mom and does not see it as a cost in terms of taking time away from her friends.

Determining *what counts as what* can be achieved in three ways: observation, third parties, and direct dialogue. To create just relationships relational partners need to be keen observers of one another's behavior as indicators of what they see as potential rewards and costs, likes and dislikes. My mother was such an observer. Christmas gifts she gave were always spot-on because all year she watched and listened to what each family member valued. In addition, third parties can be accessed to check one's own perceptions. Talking to trusted others in your social network can validate your sense of what is valued by your relational partner. Finally, direct dialogue, when characterized by openness and honesty, can provide a clear path to understanding. Note of caution: Sometimes, asking what is important to your partner can be interpreted as your inattention in the first place (in some peoples' eyes, "If you cared, you would know!"). That is why this is best done in dialogue, looking for elaboration and clarification (I elaborate on dialogue in Chapter Three: "Good Relationships.").

> *Living It Out: Take time to consider what is of value to your relational partner. If need be, for certain issues, ask! (Please note the caution discussed above.) Now, take time to consider what is of value to your own self.*

Acting Justly: What Is Most Needed?—Equity, Equality, or Need

Once you have an idea of what is valued by your partner and yourself, you are able to act in a just manner in the relationship. When engaging a specific relationship issue or problem, take time to discern what aspect of justice is most needed at this time—a response to equity, equality or need. Work by Deutsch (2006, 2011), discussed previously, suggests the following guidelines for discerning which aspects of justice are likely desired in any given situation. When one is primarily comparing

TABLE 2.2 Types of Relational Justice

Type of Justice Sample Behavior	
Distributive Justice	
Equity	distributing tangible resources
Equality	focusing on relational qualities like love and intimacy
Need	one partner is in greater need; often this is reciprocal, resulting in equity over time
Processual Justice	
relationship rules	"we always discuss big purchases"
interaction qualities	"we treat one another with respect"
fair relationship	"I think we both try to do the best for each other"

personal gains (rewards) to energy or effort expended (costs), justice is often viewed in terms of equity, the ratio of rewards to costs. That is, you are likely to feel that your relationship with a friend is just if his ratio of relational rewards to costs matches your own (or, essentially, if the one who puts the most into the relationship gets the most out of it).

Equality issues focus on equivalent rewards and costs. This perspective emerges most frequently when regarding relational themes related to love and intimacy. Partners may be satisfied with equity regarding certain themes at certain times; however, for relational issues such as closeness and commitment, often equity is not as satisfying. Jon loves restoring his 1957 Corvette, and Rebecca loves old books, so together the relationship feels equitable, balanced. But when Rebecca began putting more emotional energy into the relationship, even though she was getting more out of it, she felt the relationship was out of balance. Rebecca wanted their experience of closeness and commitment in the relationship to be equal. Finding out that you are more invested in the relationship than your partner feels unfair (unless the relationship was established on this basis).

When justice manifests as *need*, partners are less concerned with equity and equality (although these may be manifest over time—I help you when you are in need, you help me when I am). They typically understand what is fair or just as related to broader relationship goals; for example, they are both committed to the physical, psychological, and spiritual health of the other. In this context, when an individual is in need, the partner is willing to invest in her with no promise of equity or equality. The need principle often surfaces in situations where it appears that the person in need has little control over the situation (for example, financial problems due to economic downturn or the discovery of cancer).

> *Living It Out: Determine if your current situation is one where justice is primarily based on equity, equality, and/or need. How might this affect how you will pursue a just outcome in this situation?*

Acting Justly: Show Respect

Determining equality, equity, and need is essential to maintaining just relationships. However, most central to experiencing a long-term sense of relationship fairness is to pay close attention to fair process. Fair process (processual justice) encompasses relationship rules (or informal norms), the nature of relationship interactions, and the overall perception of the relationship itself. A common thread running through these fair process elements is respect.

Respect is most consistently exhibited by relational partners who believe they are of equal value in the relationship. This essential belief creates a relationship mythology that maintains the partners' alliance. I'm using myth, here, as an ideology or belief that reveals something *true* about a particular culture, specifically for us, a relational culture. For example, marriage researchers have found that happy couples tend to make positive attributions about their partner's behavior (Bradbury & Fincham, 1990; McNulty, O'Mara, & Karney, 2008). Creating a shared positive relationship mythology (e.g., "Our relationship is unique") can help us live consistently with what we value. As such, as I have argued elsewhere (Kelley, 2015), holding a justice myth about one's relationship ("Overall, we treat one another fairly") can create relational space for just interactions to take place.

Just interactions are characterized by respectful behavior and the primary elements of dialogue (discussed in Chapter Three: "Good Relationships") are largely based on treating one another with respect. As Deutsch (2011) puts forth, in moral relationships we protect and respect one another. Genuine dialogue creates an emotionally safe environment where partners are treated as equally valued participants in the relationship.

> *Living It Out: Create a mythology of respect for your relationship (e.g., "Even when we disagree we respect one another"). Think of at least one way to remind one another of this "truth" about your relationship.*
>
> *Living It Out: How can you treat your partner with respect, even when you are hurt, angry, or disappointed? Think of a time in the last month when you did not respond to your partner with respect. How can you change your behavior to respond more respectfully next time?*

Acting Justly: Take a Nonviolence Approach

Nonviolence is an approach that values the innate humanity of our relational partners. When we respond nonviolently to our children, friends, and lovers we respect them as persons. Rosenberg (2015) suggests nonviolent communication involves empathy and appropriate expression of feelings, using requests rather than making demands, and responding in ways that minimize feelings of being judged. It is helpful, at times, to create relationship rules to keep our goal of nonviolent communication specific and concrete—"Speak honestly," "Don't interrupt," "No yelling,"

"No sex outside of marriage." One function of these guidelines is to ensure just actions and interactions . . . even when we don't feel like acting in a just manner! As we will discuss in Chapter Four: "Love Relationships," just relationships ideally come from the heart. But, none of us lives perfectly in a way that reflects our deepest desires, so relationship rules help guide us when we are tempted to stray from our guiding principles.

> *Living It Out: Find time for you and your partner to discuss how you can embrace nonviolence in your relationship. To start, create two specific guidelines that will help each of you feel affirmed and respected (e.g., no name-calling).*
>
> *Living It Out: Most relationship partners have goals for what they want to have or achieve, but few have goals for the relationship itself. Find a safe, nonconflict to negotiate relationship rules that reflect what you and your relational partner desire for the relationship. (For example: Let's take a break, when our conversation gets heated, to make certain we keep speaking to one another with respect.)*

Case 2.1

Regina and Gustavo have hit the proverbial seven-year slump. They got married during a time when their friends were marrying and now they have two children, and are in their early 30s trying to keep their careers going. As a nurse Regina makes more money than Gustavo, but when they began having children Regina started working part time in order to stay at home with the kids, and Gustavo continued to work as a software programmer. Although Regina loves being a mom, she misses playing a more significant role at the hospital where she works. Lately, Regina and Gustavo's conversations have gone something like this:

Regina: I'm thinking about taking a couple extra shifts this month.

Gustavo: That doesn't make any sense. We're okay financially, so there's really no reason for you to add this additional pressure.

Regina: Well, I would like to have a few extra dollars, but . . . I guess I just really would like to do it, you know?

Gustavo: I don't know. We're already busy and don't get enough time together. My mom didn't work outside the home at all, and it was great for us kids.

Regina: Well, my mom did work outside the home and I turned out fine. It's just . . . it's just that you get everything. I mean, you're working on your career, you get to come home most days to me and the kids. It just doesn't seem fair to me that I'm stuck at home.

Gustavo: You're not *stuck* at home. I thought this was what you wanted. It's all balanced—you work mostly in the home, I work mostly out of the home. Equal.

Regina: You're missing the point. I miss some of the challenges of my career.

Gustavo: I don't think you can really call nursing a career. It's been a great help, but it's not like my job.

Regina: You're just being selfish!

Gustavo: You're just jealous because I got a bonus this month!

Regina: Forget it. You'll never really understand me.

Gustavo: Whatever.

Processing . . .

1. How does justice show up in this story?
2. What aspects of this situation are distributive justice issues based on equity, equality, or need?
3. How do process elements affect the eventual outcome in this case?
4. What words reveal Regina and Gustavo's perspective on what is just (fair) in the relationship?

Case 2.2

Guicho, an old gang leader who had been in our group for years, came to me one day so angry that he was literally shaking. He was serving as a counselor for Kids' Club. Anyway, he got close to me and he said, "Wayne, one of the kids in my small group—I went up to him, I put my arm on his shoulder, and that kid spit in my face." And I said, "Yeah, well, that'll happen." And he said, "You don't understand. In my gang I would not talk about this. I would just say the word and this boy would be dead. He would not be dead tomorrow. He'd be dead, now! No one does this to me!" It took me a moment to grasp what my friend was telling me. I could see the dark rage in his eyes, but I also knew the changes in his heart, so I talked to him about how we spit in others' faces every day, by the way we respond to them. It went against everything he knew and understood, but he made it through that year with that young boy.

More than ten years later I was interviewing a young man who had grown up in our organization. He told me he liked working with "the really tough kid, the kid that was like me. I want the kid that nobody wants." He went on, "Today I walked up to one of my kids, and I put my arm around him, and he spit in my face. And I remembered when I was 9, I spit in my leader's face." And I was amazed and I said, "You're the kid that spit in Guicho's face. You're the kid!" I couldn't wait to get home and call Guicho and tell him, "I found the boy who spit in your face and guess what happened to him today? One of his kids spit in his face, and he did what you did. He remembered you and stood and took it, and isn't going to give up on that kid." My old friend and I talked on the phone with tears in our eyes for the tremendous miracle that day. (As told by Wayne. Adapted from "Turning the Other Cheek," in *The Relentless Pursuit: Stories of God's Hope, Love and Grace in the Neighborhood* by Sherman, 2007.)

Processing . . .

1. How does justice show up in this story? What was of value to each of the people in this story?
2. Based on equity, equality, or need, how are the situations presented here related to distributive justice?
3. How do process elements, especially respect, affect the eventual outcome in this case?

References

Bradbury, T. N., & Fincham, F. D. (1990). Attributions in marriage: Review and critique. *Psychological Bulletin, 107*, 3–33.

Deutsch, M. (2006). Justice and conflict. In M. Deutsch, P. T. Coleman, & E. C. Marcus (Eds.), *The handbook of conflict resolution: Theory and practice* (pp. 43–68). San Francisco: Jossey-Bass.

Deutsch, M. (2011). Justice and conflict. In P. T. Coleman (Ed.), *Conflict, interdependence, and justice: The intellectual legacy of Morton Deutsch* (pp. 95–118). New York: Springer.

Kelley, D. L. (2015). Just marriage. In V. R. Waldron & D. L. Kelley (Eds.), *Moral talk across the lifespan* (pp. 75–94). New York: Peter Lang.

Lerner, M. J. (1980). *The belief in a just world: A fundamental delusion.* New York: Plenum.

Lerner, M. J. (2002). Pursuing the justice motive. In M. Ross & D. T. Miller (Eds.), *The justice motive in everyday life* (pp. 10–40). Cambridge: Cambridge University Press.

Lind, E. A. (2001). Fairness heuristic theory: Justice judgments as pivotal cognitions in organizational relations. In J. Greenberg & R. Cropanzano (Eds.), *Advances in organizational justice* (pp. 56–89). San Francisco, CA: New Lexington Press.

McNulty, J. K., O'Mara, E. M., & Karney, B. R. (2008). Benevolent cognitions as a strategy of relationship maintenance: "Don't sweat the small stuff". . . .but it is not all small stuff. *Journal of Personality and Social Psychology, 94*, 631–646.

Rosenberg, M. B. (2015). *Nonviolent communication: A language of life.* Encinitas, CA: PuddleDancer Press.

Sherman, A. L. (2007). *The relentless pursuit: Stories of God's hope, love, and grace in the neighborhood.* Colorado Springs, CO: Dawson Media.

USA Today. (2014). http://www.usatoday.com/story/news/politics/2014/12/21/obama-cnn-hack-attack-north-korea-sony/20723053/

3

GOOD RELATIONSHIPS

We are moral beings. Social justice is embedded in this basic assumption. Inherent in the idea of justice is that some behaviors are better than others, and, most significantly, that all people have the "right" to be treated in particularly moral ways. In this sense, the United States' Declaration of Independence is a moral document as it makes certain moral assumptions—all people are created equal and have the right to life, liberty, and the pursuit of happiness (for other examples, search the internet for the *United Nations Human Rights Council,* the *Nuremberg Code,* the *World Medical Association Declaration of Helsinki,* and the *Navajo Nation Human Research Code*). At an interpersonal level, when we make statements like, "You can't do that!" "You owe me," "Don't treat him that way!" or "I should have . . ." we are assuming some behaviors are *right* or *wrong, good* or *bad*—we are operating according to moral standards. As we discussed in Chapter Two: "Just Relationships," all people have a sense of justice in their relationships. And, although what is considered just varies by relationship and culture, to pursue socially just relationships is to pursue moral relationships, or what one considers "good" relationships.

Moral development is an essential part of our personal relationships and occurs throughout our entire lives (Waldron & Kelley, 2015). Essentially, as we live out our interpersonal relationships, we work out what it means to live a "good" life. Although there is considerable variability as to how intentional this process is, moral learning starts early on as parents, grandparents, and other primary caregivers attempt to pass on moral values to us as children and grandchildren—"Don't hit your brother," "Share with your sister" (Socha & Eller, 2015; Waldron, Danaher, Goman, Piemonte, & Kloeber, 2015). As we grow older we find that various moral issues are negotiated as part of the bedrock of our relationships—"You promised!" "Don't ever lie to me," "No dating other people," "I need to know I can count on you." In many ways, our close relationships become moral breeding grounds for learning cultural and relational values, and promoting "honesty, caring, loyalty, self-knowledge, patience, and empathy" (LaFollette, 1996, p. 197).

Not only are these "good" elements negotiated while building our relationships, but they are often renegotiated when relational transgressions occur (Guerrero & Cole, 2015; Waldron & Kelley, 2008). Because many of the implicit and explicit rules that guide relationships are moral in nature ("You should always tell the truth"), violations of these rules take on a moral character and so do the subsequent relationship talks after the violation.

It's important to note what may be the obvious: negotiation of moral values varies by individual relationship, family, and culture. For example, students in my course on inner-city families often grapple with the idea of *loyalty*. They are generally surprised to find that certain young women, coming from low-income urban areas, value being pregnant as an unmarried adolescent. The pregnancy isn't typically planned, but the resultant mother-child relationship represents a promise that can be kept, "an opportunity to prove one's worth" (Edin & Kefalas, 2005, p. 6). Many of my students, who spent their adolescence trying *not* to get pregnant, struggle to understand this value system. However, once they hear the stories of the young women who come to my class, they often experience the beginnings of understanding and empathy.

Although there are differences in the development of specific moral codes, there are commonalities that cut across most relationships and cultures. For example, Deutsch (2011) proposes that the moral orientation of our personal relationships is based on considering others, not just one's self, and that the relationship experience is fair for all partners:

> Not only is one personally affected; so are the other participants in the relationship, because its value underpinnings are being undermined. The various participants in a relationship have the mutual obligation to respect and protect the framework of social norms that define what is to be considered as fair or unfair in the interactions and outcomes of the participants.
>
> *(p. 256–258)*

In essence, once you are "in relationship" with someone (as friends, romantic partners, family) you and your relationship partner have a mutual obligation to "respect and protect" what the two of you have negotiated as fair or unfair in the relationship. Vince Waldron and I have presented *Negotiated Morality Theory* as a means of understanding this complex process.

Negotiated Morality Theory

Our long program of forgiveness research and practice has made it clear that people often understand relationship transgressions as "wrong," "shouldn't have happened," and "bad" (Kelley, 2012; Waldron & Kelley, 2008). In essence, they experience their relationship pain within a greater moral context. The offensive behavior isn't simply irritating or even hurtful, and the moral nature of the transgression often intensifies the response from the one who is offended ("I trusted you!"). *Negotiated Morality Theory* (*NMT*; Waldron & Kelley, 2008) gives us a starting point as to how this process works.

NMT: Assumptions

Negotiated Morality Theory (NMT) describes theoretical assumptions underlying the development of an interpersonal moral ethic, and inherent moral functions of communication behavior (in particular, forgiveness communication that is discussed at length in Chapter 12: "Forgiveness—Choosing How You Want to Live"). Following, I have consolidated and modified the eight theoretical assumptions of NMT into four basic assumptions that influence how we negotiate an interpersonal moral ethic.

First, *we view our relationships in light of our values.* One participant couple in our forgiveness research (Waldron & Kelley, 2008) had to deal with forgiveness over the fact that the wife, twice, got them into deep financial trouble. The husband told us that he didn't have to forgive her for not handling money well, he had to forgive her for not being honest about their financial trouble. The real issue was one of values—honesty. Our values are the essential principles and standards by which we determine what we think is right or good or best behavior in any given relationship or situation. Values are, to a limited extent, present in infants (Bloom, 2013), and then learned implicitly (e.g., modeling) and explicitly (e.g., direct teaching) through our families, personal experiences, and greater culture. As Bloom (2010) states so eloquently, "It is the insights of rational individuals that make a truly universal and unselfish morality something that our species can aspire to."

Second, *not all values are created equal.* We are most highly motivated to act in moral ways when values are part of our greater community, are personally valued, are valued by our relational partners, and have been held for a long period of time. It is more difficult to act in a manner consistent with our personal values when our relational partners and social support network do not hold to, or support, the same values. If you were raised in a family and small community that primarily values heterosexual marriage, your choice to move in with your partner could be difficult, even though the Supreme Court just voted to legalize gay marriage.

Third, *we create and maintain relational moral ethics through dialogue.* While many relational values are simply assumed and never directly discussed, the importance of a particular moral ethic may lead to direct discussion of its importance—parent to child: "If we are going to trust you while we're gone, you have to be totally honest with us," or one dating partner to another: "I need to make sure we're on the same page. We're not going to see other people, right?" The breaking of a moral code can also generate discussion—between dating partners: "I didn't know that being 'exclusive' meant that I couldn't text with my ex," or high school student to his mentor: "Because you said I could come to your apartment any time, I thought you'd be cool with it if I drank a couple of your beers until you got home."

Fourth, *threats to our relational values (relational moral ethic) result in an emotional response.* As we will discuss more fully in Chapter 12: "Forgiveness: Choosing How You Want to Live," when one's own or partner's behavior is inconsistent with negotiated relational values, it precipitates an emotional response. Emotional responses to transgressions can include hurt, anger, frustration, disappointment, jealousy, embarrassment, and sadness (Guerrero & Cole, 2015). Triggered emotional responses are useful as indicators that something of importance needs to be dealt with. However, the extreme levels of arousal that drive certain emotions may also compromise one's ability to engage in productive dialogue and problem solving (more to come on this in Chapter Eleven: "Engaging Conflict"). Consider, for example, Adam and Seth, two roommates who used humor to negotiate confidentiality in their relationship, "What happens in the room, stays in the room," but then didn't speak to each other for two weeks after Adam contacted Seth's parents because Seth was into some hard drugs and going to drop out of school. Whether or not you believe what Seth did was the "right" call, his violation of their moral code heightened emotions to such an extent that they didn't talk to each other for two weeks.

NMT: Functions of Moral Communication

Like all communication, moral communication fulfills certain functions in relationships. Another way to think about functions of moral communication is to ask, "What is this used for? What is its result?" Perhaps the foremost moral function of relational communication is defining each relationship's unique moral standards. As discussed previously, at certain points in their relational history, partners typically engage in dialogue that blends cultural and personal values into a joint relationship moral ethic. Central to the development of the relationship moral ethic is an understanding of how partners are treated fairly within the relationship (procesual justice). This includes how resources will be distributed equitably, but more importantly focuses on fair process in the relationship, including the development of fair relationship rules that create an emotionally safe space for partners and equal participation (e.g., no interrupting), quality partner interaction (e.g., demonstrating respect for one another), and the creation of a relationship ideology based on equality and respect (see Chapter Two: "Just Relationships").

The functions of moral communication stand out when one party perceives that the negotiated relationship ethic has been violated. For example, in our interviews with long-term married couples, after a relationship transgression partners sensed the need to communicate about a variety of moral functions, including: establish accountability, deal with moral tensions, restore relational justice, create hope through imagining a moral future, affirm one's own self, redirect hostility, increase safety and certainty, find closure, grant forgiveness, and possibly negotiate reconciliation (Waldron & Kelley, 2008).

Moral Dialogue: More Than Talk about Rules

Morality is often negotiated and experienced through dialogue. However, moral dialogue is about much more than simply talking about rules and guidelines. Let's take a deeper look.

Dialogue intended to negotiate an objective understanding of moral standards in a relationship has been termed technical dialogue (Buber, 1967). For example, when roommates discuss boundaries regarding their possessions, they are involved in technical moral dialogue ("It's not 'right' to borrow my car without asking" or "Anything in the refrigerator can be eaten by anyone"). However, dialogue, in and of itself, can be an experience of morality, not merely a means of discussing guidelines for morality. Baxter (2004), in a discussion of Bakhtin's (1990) perspective on dialogue, states that dialogue is the means to address the "moral and ethical responsibility that individuals bear toward others in order to 'author' or complete them. . . . Parties owe each other the opportunity for their selves to become" (Baxter, 2004, p. 118). Similarly, Buber (1967) tells us that *genuine dialogue* is "whether spoken or silent—where each of the participants really has in mind the other or others in their present and particular being and turns to them with the intention of establishing a living mutual relation between himself and them" (p. 113). In this sense, dialogue is actually a place where morality is experienced, where we become more fully human—*to be in genuine dialogue with someone is to treat her morally.*

Essential to the process of genuine dialogue is that each partner connects with the other. There is no room here for simplistic ideas of unity, where individuals ignore their differences in order to achieve simple solutions or false peace. As Baxter (2011) states, "Dialogue . . . is a process in which unity and difference, in some form, are at play, both with and against one another" (p. 32). In fact, within the context of genuine dialogue, experiencing differences with one another may actually lead to an increased sense of unity and closeness. An example of this for me occurred a couple years ago when my wife and I were in counseling—often we felt most connected when we honestly shared our differences with one another. As hard as it was, safely engaging each other created a space for us to individually grow, which created a better foundation for our relationship.

Essential to becoming a socially just relational partner is recognition that genuine dialogue goes beyond simple problem-solving conversation. At its finest, dialogue becomes a way of creating and touching our full humanity. As Manusov (2015) observes, "it is often the way we make sense of things *coming into a relationship* that matters most." Manusov's own work lends itself to greater understanding of genuine dialogue as she suggests that mindfulness (awareness and acceptance, without judgment, of experiences as they exist in the present moment; Brown & Ryan, 2003; Manusov, 2015) is a moral way of being with another person as it allows us, free from judgment, "to be more fully with another person and ourselves *just as we are.*" To return to the preceding example of my wife and I, honestly sharing our differences, without judgment, created a safe place where we were individually affirmed and felt connected to one another. Thus, genuine dialogue is a mindful and moral way for partners to experience "communion and the ground of self-discovery" (Matson & Montagu, 1967, p. viii).

Building "Good" Relationships

Social justice in interpersonal relationships is achieved by creating moral relationships, built on the essential principles of dialogue. Through dialogue we negotiate our relationship moral ethic—what we mutually see as good. And, when mindfully engaged, we actually experience a moral moment as we genuinely connect with one another. Following, I consider dialogue as a means of healthy negotiation, and then explore mindfulness as a means for creating moral experience through dialogue.

Dialogue: Negotiating What Is Good

The creation of your relationship's moral ethic takes place largely through dialogue (Baxter, Pederson, & Norwood, 2015; Haste & Abrahams, 2008; Waldron & Kelley, 2008). The following is designed to help you negotiate what you and your partner think is good within the relationship (your relationship ethic). I begin with *Four Dialogue Principles* that are essential to guide the process, then focus on *Three Dialogue Acts* that help us understand what constructive dialogue actually looks like.

Four Dialogue Principles

Relationships based on genuine dialogue are characterized by a "turn toward the other" (Buber, 1967, p. 115). Based on work by Baxter and Montgomery (1996), I offer four principles that help us make this turn: embrace contradiction, respect other voices in addition to one's own, maintain ongoing conversation, and be creative (see Baxter & Montgomery, 1996).

Embracing contradiction encourages us to lay aside *either/or* approaches to communication (either A or B; either you are right or I am right) and embrace *both/and* approaches that recognize the inherent value of both parties' perspectives. Contradiction can actually provide vitality in relationships as partners continue to grow and learn with each other.

> *Living It Out: What can you learn from your partner's perspective (even if you disagree with him or her)?*

Respecting voices other than one's own creates a relational mindset focused on what each relational partner has to offer, rather than arguing for unilateral decision-making and control. This perspective embraces each individual as the partners work together toward joint decisions. In this light, Baxter and Montgomery (1996) state that, "a couple's behavior is interactionally competent when it is judged to be sensitive to each partner's logic" (pp. 199–200). Or, put another way, competent relational communication takes into account how and what the other person thinks.

> *Living It Out: Think about an issue where you and your partner hold differing opinions. How can you show respect for your partner's thinking and work together to create a joint decision regarding this issue?*

Maintaining ongoing conversation inherently excludes behaviors that tend to shut down dialogue, such as violence. Violent behaviors are generally understood as verbal or nonverbal actions intended to harm another person (Spitzberg, 2009). As related to dialogue, violence typically limits choices for partners and stunts equal participation. Similarly, distributive (e.g., faulting the other person and hostile joking) and avoidant (e.g., topic shifts and denials of conflict) actions work against open dialogue and are associated with lower interactional and relational quality (Baxter & Montgomery, 1996).

> *Living It Out: Make an assessment of what types of behaviors might be shutting down open dialogue in your relationship. This week, pick one behavior that you can work on changing.*

Being creative is one of my favorite aspects of dialogue. It recognizes that our social existence is ever changing. That is, our relationships are always in process. Partner dialogue at its best includes thinking outside the box in ways that help the relationship move progressively toward a moral and just future. As Baxter and Montgomery (1996) note, "To interact fully and inquisitively within a relational context means to be dyadically proactive, imaginative, and figuratively reaching forward" (p. 205).

> *Living It Out: How are you and your partner responding creatively to keep your relationship moving forward in ways that benefit you both? Are there areas of your relationship that could use more creativity?*

Three Dialogue Acts

We've just overviewed four general principles that guide dialogue. Following are three specific communication acts that naturally proceed from these principles: systemic questioning, appreciative inquiry, and shared hypothesizing (Baxter, 2011; Pearce & Littlejohn, 1997). *Systemic questioning* invites relationship participants to wonder about their own interactions, shifting focus from individual needs and wants to the shared process of negotiation. It takes the emphasis off of *me* and shifts it to the relationship and connection between me and my relationship partner. *Appreciative inquiry* represents a significant shift from the type of questioning that searches for information in order to defend one's own position. Refreshingly, appreciative inquiry shifts participants' focus from negative to positive elements within the relationship by searching for "hidden virtues and positive resources" (Pearce & Littlejohn, 1997, p. 201). These first two elements create a positive, other-centered environment where partners can *jointly hypothesize*, creatively and informatively speculate, regarding relationship issues. When done well, partners eventually find themselves in new relational spaces (further discussed in Chapter Five: "Interpersonal Advocacy: Creating Spaces") that allow for fresh ideas and practices to emerge.

> *Living It Out: Together, take time to examine the nature of your relationship's interactions. View individual needs as part of joint relationship goals. Build on the good in the relationship. Generate new possibilities for the future.*

Dialogue: Being Present

Mindfulness may aid the process of dialogue (Pearce & Pearce, 2000) and create a moral experience when relationship partners connect at deeper levels. Manusov (2015) identifies four elements typically associated with mindfulness: observing, describing, acting with awareness, and accepting without judgment. For our purposes, I've adapted these to focus on dialogue in interpersonal relationships. *Observing* involves attending to internal and external stimuli. As discussed previously, this involves being aware of one's own, and one's partner's, thoughts, feelings, and needs. *Describing* is labeling and defining "present-moment stimuli and experiences." The focus here is on what's happening in the *now* between interactants. This keeps the dialogue unencumbered by power moves that are oriented toward the past or future. *Acting with awareness* is the capacity to focus attention on one thing in the present moment in order to keep dialogue free from extraneous distractions. *Withholding judgment* refrains from evaluation of either partner's behaviors. Judgment leads to defensiveness and closedness, whereas honest observation encourages genuine dialogue. When practiced together, these four elements create a sense of presence between partners that facilitates understanding that is free from judgment. In essence, it creates a safe space to be "human" with another human being (a *moral way of being*) and to negotiate one's relationship moral ethic.

> *Living It Out: Carefully, and nonjudgmentally, observe your partner's behavior and your own thoughts and behavior. How is observing without judgment different from your "normal" experience?*
>
> *Living It Out: During any given interaction, focus on what is happening in the "now"—limit thinking about the past or future (that might be used to gain power or fuel resentment), and focus only on what is happening during the interaction.*
>
> *Living It Out: Be open. Focus on understanding. Don't be judgmental.*

Case 3.1

John and Sameer have been friends since childhood. In high school Sameer began dating Katie. John dated a variety of girls. As best friends, Sameer and John double-dated often. John, Sameer, and Katie all ended up at the same university, about two hours from their hometown. Sameer and Katie continued to date each other, and John continued to date a variety of women. However, at the end of their sophomore year, Sameer and Katie broke up. Because they'd been dating since high school, Sameer felt like he needed to experience other people before he and Katie got more serious. During their "relationship break," John and Katie were at home for the summer and began to hang out, while Sameer stayed at school for an internship. In the fall, when everyone was back on campus for their junior year, Sameer sensed awkwardness from Katie. Eventually, it came out that Katie and John were seeing each other. Later, Sameer and John had the following discussion:

John:	Hey, Man! What's up?
Sameer:	Not much.
John:	You sure? You seem out of it.
Sameer:	Well, I just talked to Katie. She told me.
John:	Told you what?
Sameer:	That the two of you are going out.
John:	So?
Sameer:	So, you just don't do that to a friend.
John:	Do what? You two weren't dating anymore.
Sameer:	Dude, you knew how long we had dated and that we were on a break. That's not cool.
John:	What's not cool about it? I always liked Katie but kept my distance because of our friendship. Once you were done, I wasn't going to let some other guy start hitting on her.
Sameer:	Who told you we were done?
John:	You did! You said you wanted to date other people to "see what's out there."
Sameer:	Yeah, but that didn't mean we were finished.
John:	Look, man, you're seriously messed up. All I know is that Katie is interested in me, now. You lost your chance.
Sameer:	You are such an ass! This is why I never really trusted you. If you want something, you just do what you want without thinking about anyone else.
John:	You are out of control. I'm out!
Sameer:	Perfect. Well, I am going to talk to Katie, and I am going to tell her how you screwed me over!

Processing

1. Discuss why this conflict can be considered a moral conflict.
2. To what extent do Sameer and John respect and protect one another?
3. Which of the moral functions (described in the chapter) were present, or needed to be brought out more directly, in this interaction?
4. Do Sameer and John use any dialogue acts (described in the chapter)?
5. Describe how the following dialogue principles could have been used in this case: be willing to embrace contradiction, respect other voices besides one's own, maintain ongoing conversation, be creative.

Case 3.2

LaShanna is upper middle class, married with three children, and volunteers with a variety of community organizations. She is mentoring Debbie, a single mom, who is 19 with two children (ages 2 and 4), on financial assistance, and works part time. Debbie has a sister, Mercy, also with two children. Mercy has had multiple jobs in the last year, largely due to her drug habit. The last time Debbie and LaShanna got together, Debbie hesitantly told LaShanna that she doesn't know what to do because her sister badly needs some money to keep the electricity on in her apartment. Debbie has the money, but if she helps her sister she will be late paying her own rent, and she has been working on improving her credit rating so she can eventually buy a more reliable used car. Debbie and LaShanna's conversation about this issue was brief and to the point:

Debbie: I'm not sure what to do. My sister needs money again, to keep her electricity turned on.

LaShanna: Debbie, I know you love your sister, but the most loving thing you can do for her is teach her responsibility by not giving her the money.

Debbie: But I have to do it for her kids.

LaShanna: You can't be there every time her kids are going to be uncomfortable. Besides, we went through that book on finances together and if you're late on your rent it could affect your credit score.

Debbie: But, she is family. That just isn't right.

LaShanna: Debbie, it's not like this is the first time. If you love your sister you need to tell her, "No."

Debbie: (silence; later that day she gives her sister a check to pay her electric)

Processing

1. What are the various moral issues/values in this conflict?
2. To what extent do LaShanna and Debbie respect and protect one another?
3. Which of the moral functions (described in the chapter) were present, or needed to be brought out more directly, in this interaction?
4. Do Debbie and LaShanna use any dialogue acts (described in the chapter) to move toward genuine dialogue?
5. Rewrite the dialogue in this case. How can you help LaShanna be more *present* or *mindful* to Debbie? What dialogue principles and acts could help turn this conversation into a genuine dialogue?

References

Bakhtin, M. M. (1990). *Art and answerability: Early philosophical works by M. M. Bakhtin* (M. Holquist & V. Liapunov, Eds.; V. Liapunov, Trans.). Austin: University of Texas Press.

Baxter, L. A. (2004). Dialogues of relating. In R. Anderson, L. A. Baxter, & K. N. Cissna (Eds.), *Dialogue: Theorizing difference in communication studies* (pp. 107–124). Thousand Oaks, CA: Sage.

Baxter, L. A. (2011). *Voicing relationships: A dialogic perspective*. Los Angeles: Sage.

Baxter, L. A., & Montgomery, B. M. (1996). *Relating: Dialogues and dialectics*. New York: The Guilford Press.

Baxter, L. A., Pederson, S. N., & Norwood, K. M. (2015). Negotiating relational moral-ity: Poetic justice. In V. R. Waldron & D. L. Kelley (Eds.), *Moral talk across the lifespan* (pp. 117–135). New York: Peter Lang.

Bloom, P. (2010, May 5). The moral life of babies. *The New York Times Magazine*. http://www.nytimes.com/2010/05/09/magazine/09babies-t.html?pagewanted=all&_r=0

Bloom, P. (2013). *Just babies: The origins of good and evil*. New York: Crown Publishers.

Brown, K. W., & Ryan, R. M. (2003). The benefits of being present: Mindfulness and its role in psychological well-being. *Journal of Personality and Social Psychology, 84*, 822–848.

Buber, M. (1967). Between man and man: The realms. In F. W. Matson & A. Montagu (Eds.), *The human dialogue: Perspectives on communication* (pp. 113–117). New York: The Free Press.

Deutsch, M. (2011). Justice and conflict. In P. T. Coleman (Ed.), *Conflict, interdependence, and justice: The intellectual legacy of Morton Deutsch* (pp. 95–118). New York: Springer.

Edin, K., & Kefalas, M. (2005). *Promises I can keep: Why poor women put motherhood before marriage*. Berkeley: University of California Press.

Guerrero, L. K., & Cole, M. (2015). Moral standards, emotions, and communication asso-ciated with relational transgressions in dating relationships. In V. Waldron & D. Kelley (Eds.), *Moral talk across the lifespan* (pp. 155–182). New York: Peter Lang.

Haste, H., & Abrahams, S. (2008). Morality, culture and the dialogic self: Taking cultural pluralism seriously. *Journal of Moral Education, 37*(3), 377–394. http://www.tandfonline.com/.../03057240802227502

Kelley, D. L. (2012). *Marital communication*. Cambridge, UK: Polity.

LaFollette, H. (1996). *Personal relationships: Love, identity, and morality*. Oxford, UK: Blackwell.

Manusov, V. (2015). Mindfulness as morality: Awareness, nonjudgment, and nonreactivity in couples' communication. In V. R. Waldron & D. L. Kelley (Eds.), *Moral talk across the lifespan* (pp. 183–201). New York: Peter Lang.

Matson, F. W., & Montagu, A. (1967). Introduction: The unfinished revolution. In F. W. Mat-son & A. Montagu (Eds.), *The human dialogue: Perspectives on communication* (pp. 113–117). New York: The Free Press.

Pearce, W. B., & Littlejohn, S. W. (1997). *Moral conflict: When social worlds collide*. Thou-sand Oaks, CA: Sage.

Pearce, W. B., & Pearce, K. A. (2000). Combining passions and abilities: Toward dialogic virtuosity. *Southern Communication Journal, 65*, 161–175.

Socha, T. J., & Eller, A. (2015). Parent/Caregiver-child communication and moral develop-ment: Towards a conceptual foundation of an ecological model of lifespan communica-tion and good relationships. In V. R. Waldron & D. L. Kelley (Eds.), *Moral talk across the lifespan* (pp.15–34). New York: Peter Lang.

Spitzberg, B. H. (2009). Aggression, violence, and hurt in close relationships. In A. Vange-listi (Ed.), *Feeling hurt in close relationships* (pp. 209–232). New York: Cambridge Uni-versity Press.

Waldron, V., Danaher, J., Goman, C., Piemonte, N., & Kloeber, D. (2015). Which parental messages about morality are accepted by emerging adults? In V. Waldron & D. Kelley (Eds.), *Moral talk across the lifespan* (pp. 155–182). New York: Peter Lang.

Waldron, V., & Kelley, D. (2015). *Moral talk across the lifespan*. New York: Peter Lang.

Waldron, V. R., & Kelley, D. L. (2008). *Communicating forgiveness*. Thousand Oaks, CA: Sage.

4

LOVE RELATIONSHIPS

Social justice is, first and foremost, social. Justice can really only be understood in the context of relationship. As I presented in Chapter Two: "Just Relationships," while distribution of resources, effort, and relationship consequences is fundamental, it is the processual justice elements (being treated with respect, viewing the overall relationship as fair) that drives relational partners' justice experience in the long run. Essentially, *just* distribution can only be maintained, over time, through *just* process. In the following pages, I take this perspective even farther. I make the argument that in interpersonal relationships, long-term, stable, *just process* is the result of, what I term, *full love*. Love may sound like the exact opposite of justice. But, I believe mature loving relationships actually create lasting venues for relational justice. Imagine a world where everyone was only out for themselves. Where you had to constantly manage, and cajole, and coerce every person to try to get them to act in a fair manner. Exhausting. Impossible. Or, as C. S. Lewis (1946) describes it in *The Great Divorce* . . . hell. What's love got to do with it? Everything! To explore this perspective, let's start by looking at the relationship dilemma that confronts us all—vulnerability.

The Universal Dilemma: Vulnerability

A central dilemma of personal relationships is that interdependence creates vulnerability. As our lives become intertwined with relational partners we face "uncertainty, risk, and emotional exposure" (Brown, 2012, p. 2) that make us vulnerable to personal hurt. Social justice is all about increasing our interdependence as we build relationships based on respect and equality. Consequently, the pursuit and achievement of social justice necessarily leaves us vulnerable.

Vulnerability is the hallmark of intimacy. Thus far, we have been discussing the creation of relationships that are good and just, based on a sense of fairness and respect. Yet, as we work closely together, it is inevitable that we become increasingly known by our relational partners. Being known is the essence of intimacy. It works something like this: over time, our relationship partners gain access to us—that is, they gain more information about us, spend more social time with us, experience more physical touch with us, and begin to see our psychological and emotional makeup (Kelley, 2012). In essence, the more time we spend with others, the more we become known to them, and the more vulnerable we are—whether being known comes through conversation or astute observation.

A natural consequence of this availability is that those who know us most intimately, with whom we are closest, can hurt us most deeply. Because of this significant risk, we develop ways to protect ourselves from possible hurt. There are three common strategies used to manage the vulnerability and potential pain in our lives. The first, and perhaps most obvious, approach is to protect ourselves by not allowing others much access—as folk-rock duo Simon and Garfunkel famously put it, "I am a rock. I am an island. A rock feels no pain, and an island never cries" (Simon, 1965). Second, when it is inevitable that others are going to be exposed to parts of us that could make us vulnerable (e.g., we live in the same house together), we can attempt to manage our potential vulnerability by controlling our environment—"If I can control other people and circumstances, enough, then I won't be hurt." For example, over-involved soccer mom extraordinaire, Gladyss, knows she is not perfect, but thinks that as long as she can "make her kids turn out alright," then she's alright. Third, when we can't control others' access to ourselves and we can't control the other people in our environment, we can try to shut off our inner selves emotionally to minimize any pain that might come—"I don't get emotionally attached!"

Problems with these responses to vulnerability are multifold. First and foremost, partners lose access to one another—there is no real trust, no intimacy, simply power and emotional disconnection. This is reminiscent of the Cold War between the former Soviet Union and the United States—I only trust you so long as I know I can hurt you as badly as you hurt me. There is some practical use to this perspective in certain contexts for short periods of time. However, the obvious shortcomings are that both partners live with a constant fear that their weaknesses will eventually be discovered and exploited. The typical response to this dilemma is to invest a colossal amount of resources to ensure mutual destruction. Imagine this approach being used at a personal relationship level. Suppose I told you that my relationship with my wife was healthy because we both were confident that if one of us hurt the other, the other could retaliate with equal force. Yikes! I know these types of relationships exist, but most of us don't move into our personal relationships with this type of protection as the goal.

Another flaw of these typical responses to vulnerability is that, as much as we would like to believe otherwise, we have relatively little control over our environments and the people in them. Scholars of organizational behavior for half a century have recognized that full control of organization employees is an untenable goal. For complete control one has to have the ability to constantly monitor employees, and have the power to influence them to act in a desired manner. Modern perspectives on organizational leadership focus on creating an organizational climate where employees identify with organizational goals and are motivated by relationships within the organization (Cheney, Christensen, & Dailey, 2014). Likewise, on a more personal relationship level, parents soon realize they only have so much influence over their children. I remember the first time my youngest son told me, "No!" I thought, "Who gave you an opinion? It's my job to give you your opinions!" As children grow and develop they gain personal and external resources (e.g., jobs that make money, affirmation from coaches and teachers, advice from older siblings) that significantly change how parents are able to influence the children's thinking and behavior. Yet, parents don't lose their ability to influence their children, rather, how they influence their children shifts. Research suggests that adolescents actually do listen to their parents and count them as friends (Chapman & Werner-Wilson, 2008; Van Wel, 1994). In essence, as children grow older, effective parents move toward influence that is based on love and mutual respect, rather than controlling resources.

The point here is that the best way to create sustainable, just relationships is not through remaining emotionally aloof and attempting to enforce rules through coercive means. Sustainable long-term relationships are best developed in environments where partners are mutually committed to common goals and believe they are emotionally and physically safe. However, as nice as that might sound in theory, we are still left with the vulnerability dilemma—if we cannot manage our vulnerability through control and emotional distance, how can we make certain that we are safe?

Full Love

What I am terming *full love* creates safe spaces for relational partners (Kelley, 2012). Let me take you on a short history of love to demonstrate what I mean. Social scientists have conceptualized love from a variety of perspectives, most of them in the context of romantic relationships. Romantic love has often been understood as passionate (sexual attraction, emotional turbulence, intense communication) and companionate (quiet intimacy, shared values, predictability; Hendrick & Hendrick, 1992). Sternberg's (1986, 1997) Triangular Theory of Love includes three constituent components: intimacy, commitment, and passion. Intimacy is psychological closeness, commitment is the decisional aspect of love, and passion is the emotional/motivational aspect. Similarly, Noller's (1996) view of love highlights behavioral, cognitive, and emotional aspects. Important to our focus on social justice, she also emphasizes that mature love is characterized by both partners' concern for the growth and development of the other.

Paralleling this previous work, I have offered a model of *full love* that focuses on the creation of spaces where partners can safely grow and develop individually and relationally (Kelley, 2012). The *full love* model modifies certain love concepts, discussed by previous theorists, in order to fit a broad array of relationships (parent-child, sibling, romantic, friendship), and emphasizes that intimacy is related to love, but separate and unique. Together, love and intimacy create a safe space for partners to co-exist, deeply connecting with one another.

Full love is conceptualized as emotional bonding, commitment, and other-centeredness (Kelley, 2012). Emotional bonding refers to the deep sense of emotional connection experienced by relational partners. It includes the type of passion lovers experience, but also the passion of a mother for her child. This deep-rooted passion and desire for one another creates a sense of union between relationship partners. In social justice terms, emotional bonding is the motivational element for relational partners to work together for one another's well-being. Commitment is the cognitive aspect of love. It is the decision to love, and to maintain that love. Commitment helps separate love from infatuation of a romantic partner or a desired friend. Importantly, and essential to social justice, this aspect of love represents promise and the expectation of a long-term relationship, attempting to maintain the relationship even when times are tough. Finally, other-centeredness is a perspective change resulting from emotional bonding and relational commitment. It is made manifest through helping behavior, emotional support, and building self-esteem. In this same vein, marriage researchers Stanley, Whitton, Sadberry, Clements, and Markman (2006) propose that a sound relationship commitment leads to healthy self-sacrifice. Healthy self-sacrifice is for the "good" of both partners. It encourages individual growth and development. It should be noted that this "healthy" perspective is in sharp contrast to co-dependent relationships where individuals use "sacrifice" in an unhealthy way to keep their relational partner needing them ("I'm only okay if my partner affirms me, needs me, wants me.").

Full love provides a safe context for us to risk being in relationships characterized by interdependence and intimacy and, as such, vulnerability. Of course, there are no absolute guarantees for safeguarding our vulnerability with relational partners—when we allow ourselves to be dependent on others, and we give others access to ourselves physically, socially, and psychologically, we put ourselves in potentially vulnerable positions. But, partners who love one another with a mature, full love operate within a context of emotional connection, commitment, and willingness to sacrifice for the other, all of which serve to safeguard the relationship. This tri-fold perspective allows us the freedom to trust, creating an emotionally safe space ("I trust you as I am open and honest with you") for us to work together as truly equal partners (see Chapter Five: "Interpersonal Advocacy: Creating Spaces" for more on this idea). And, significantly, it creates a safe space where we belong.

Building Loving Relationships

Desmond Tutu (1999), in his book *No Future Without Forgiveness*, beautifully presents the idea of *Ubuntu*. Ubuntu is the basic life principle that suggests we are so interdependent on one another as human beings, so intertwined in our existence, that the best way to care for our own selves is to care for others. Listen to Archbishop Tutu's take on this:

> *Ubuntu* is very difficult to render into a Western language. It speaks of the very essence of being human . . . It is to say, "My humanity is caught up,

is inextricably bound up, in yours." We belong in a bundle of life. We say, "A person is a person through other persons." It is not, "I think therefore I am." It says rather: "I am human because I belong. I participate. I share."

(p. 31)

Individuals who experience this deep sense of connection with others and, as such, experience their own self-worth, are free to treat other persons with great respect and a lack of defensiveness. I have nothing to defend when I am comfortable with who I am. And I am comfortable with who I am, because I know I am a part of something greater than my own individual self. Again, hear Tutu's (1999) words:

> A person with *ubuntu* is open to and available to others, affirming of others, does not feel threatened that others are able and good, for he or she has a proper self-assurance that comes from knowing that he or she belongs in a greater whole and is diminished when others are humiliated or diminished, when others are tortured or oppressed, or treated as if they were less than who they are.
>
> *(p. 31)*

Tutu's description of Ubuntu is similar to what Vince Waldron and I (2008) discovered when interviewing married couples, married between 30 and 80 years—mature love creates a space for justice to be sustained over time, but respect for one another also creates a rich context for love to thrive. Creating this intertwined, loving, and safe environment involves intentionally pursuing the three aspects of full love: commitment, emotional bonding, and other-centeredness.

Commitment

Commitment is the cognitive, decisional aspect of love (Sternberg, 1997), wherein you choose to care about another person or relationship, or both. Consider the following to understand how commitment to a relationship partner and the relationship itself can vary—after a deep relationship betrayal, you might not feel very committed to your best friend and, yet, because you have known each other since grade school you might still care about maintaining the friendship ("It's a lot of years of friendship to throw away"). So, when considering commitment, we first need to do our own internal processing—"To what extent *am I* committed to this person? This relationship? To what extent *do I want to be* committed to this person? This relationship?"

Once I have decided I'm committed in some way to a relationship or person, I need to express that commitment to my partner. Canary and Stafford (1992) refer to this as maintaining your relationship through giving *assurances*. Assurances communicate to your partner that you are committed to her and the continuance of the relationship. Commitment can be demonstrated in many different ways. Of course, you can directly, verbally affirm your commitment to the relationship—"I love you," "Nothing will ever come between us," "You are my BFF! (Best Friend Forever)." You can also demonstrate commitment through future-oriented communication—"Should we buy a condo downtown?" "I'll be here for you when you get back." Demonstrating your faithfulness through behavior is a way to show commitment without words—sitting by a hospital bed; leaving a party early because your partner is not feeling well; unfriending your "ex" on Facebook. Finally, you can use acts of appreciation or service to demonstrate commitment—a thoughtful card in someone's lunch; cleaning the kitchen or other acts of service; a backrub after a hard day. (For additional ideas on showing love/commitment, see *The 5 Love Languages,* 1992, by Chapman.)

> *Living It Out: Take time to journal, or talk with a friend or counselor, to process your commitment to the other person or the relationship. Are you committed? If so, what are you committed to? (It's okay not to know this fully, at this time.)*
> *Living It Out: Which of the ways of showing assurance are you good at? Of the ones that come less naturally to you, how can you use one of them to demonstrate your commitment this week?*

Emotional Bonding

Emotional bonding is perhaps the most critical part of love for today's society. Here, I am not referring to feelings of love, but the deeper emotional connection (e.g., a parent may not "feel love," in the common use of this phrase, for a drug-addicted child who has said and done hurtful things to the family, but will likely still deeply grieve when he receives a midnight phone call about an apparent overdose). Emotional bonding has taken on a significant role regarding love because, in today's Western culture, "long-term" commitment often only lasts as long as emotional connection is present. For example, for many of us, if we quit enjoying work or we "fall out of love," we move on to the next job or relationship. Historically, this is a relatively recent change. As such, cultivating and protecting a close emotional bond with our relational partners is a significant means of safeguarding our relationships.

Co-owning information and experiences is one way we develop a deep emotional connection with our romantic partners, friends, and family. Sandra Petronio (Kelley, 2012; Petronio, 2002) has shown us that relationship participants can co-own information and experiences. When we let each other into the private spaces of our lives we begin to co-own the contents of those spaces and share responsibility for it. This process can create a deep sense of emotional connection between partners. We primarily invite people to co-own these private spaces through self-disclosure, shared experiences, and being with one another when we experience deep emotion, such as feeling fear or joy.

> *Living It Out: Plan time with your relational partner to be able to share openly and honestly about issues that are important to you. (If you don't fully trust the person you're in a relationship with, go slowly with this at first.)*

> *Living It Out: Plan meaningful and/or fun events and activities that you and your relationship partners can share together. Work at being aware of your partner during these times, and sharing in his or her experience. (Try doing something new together like giving toiletries to the homeless, learning a challenging skill, attending a political rally, or traveling somewhere you both have always wanted to visit.)*

> *Living It Out: When one of you is experiencing a deep emotional response to something, don't dismiss it or run from it. Instead stay in the emotion and explore it for a period of time. (Sit together, patiently, while one of you cries. Listen to the other's anger, without becoming defensive. Be a safe place as your partner shares about a fear they have at work.)*

Other-Centeredness

Being other-centered is the final element that creates a safe space for your partner. When I know that you understand me and will sacrifice for my good, I am now safe to share with you, or show you my true emotions, or disagree with you, or walk alongside you. When we both believe that we want the best for one another, we are truly free to create a just relationship based on fairness and respect. As Tutu describes regarding Ubuntu, these are not selfless acts. This is a change in mindset that reflects our joint knowledge that what is best for both of us is to create an environment where we can each freely grow and develop. In this sense, acting with mature love is a profoundly moral act that benefits all.

> *Living It Out: Take action this week, no matter how small, that shows your partner that you are willing to do something that she or he cares about (i.e., sacrifice for her or him). (How about putting your shoes away even though you are in a rush? Or, showing up for your child's soccer game, even though you have to work? Or, doing your dishes even though you're tired?)*

> *Living It Out: Schedule a time to talk with your partner about how to create an environment in which you both can grow freely.*

Case 4.1

Joanna was deeply depressed. Things were not going as she had hoped with Kermit. They had dated on and off for two months and, though they were free to date other people, Joanna never had. She could do little else but think about him, and in her journal she had confessed that she was "deeply in love." During a "make out" session early in the relationship Kermit had actually said, "I love you," but she hadn't heard him say the words since. Still, she clung to those three words like an emotional life preserver—"I love you." They seldom planned ahead to do things together. Mostly, Kermit would call last minute and ask if she wanted to hang out. Sometimes she would think about saying, "No," but she never did. Inevitably, they would hook-up back at his place. She didn't understand why he would treat her this way if he loved her. But, then, part of her just felt lucky to be with him.

Processing

1. Using the model of *full love,* discuss whether you think Joanna and Kermit are "in love."
2. How does commitment play a role in this case?
3. How does this case illustrate the difference between "feelings" and *emotional bonding*?
4. Would you describe Joanna's behavior as healthy self-sacrifice?
5. How are vulnerability and intimacy affected by the presence (or lack thereof) of full love in this case?

Case 4.2

Rebecca has changed living situations three times over the past seven years. She was originally removed from her home by DPS (Department of Public Safety) because, at age 6, she was left alone in her apartment when her mother spent the night passed out at a friend's house. After living in a shelter for two months, Rebecca's mother petitioned for custody, and Rebecca was allowed to return home. Six months later her addicted mother had neglected her again. This time, Rebecca was placed in a foster care home as her mom was sentenced for violating probation on drug-related charges.

Rebecca was mostly angry while at her first foster care home. The foster parents were kind and polite, but she rebelled against every rule or guideline that she could. Six months later she found herself in a new home, with new foster parents—James and Ashley Sullivan. At first, Rebecca continued to act out—angry and rebellious. But, soon she tired of that and simply became sad and sullen. Her basic needs were met at the Sullivan's, but she missed her mom and, at age 14, life finally seemed meaningless and hopeless. Depressed, Rebecca began hanging with friends who smoked pot and occasionally experimented with other drugs. A former good student, she no longer cared about school.

James and Ashley knew Rebecca's history when they agreed to serve as foster parents. They were willing to take a chance with her, even though they knew life would be hard. They had two children of their own (15 and 17), and Rebecca did not make life easy for any of them. James and Ashley tried to create a positive environment for her, but positive admonitions ("We are so glad you are here," "You're really good at math!") seemed to have no effect on Rebecca. However, James and Ashley didn't want to quit. They were committed to working through the hard stuff no matter how long it took.

One night Rebecca was brought back to the house by police. She had been riding in a car with some older high school girls—the driver was stoned and had been arrested. Rebecca knew what this meant—the "talk." Ashley and James would tell her how they had tried, but it just wasn't working out. Deep down she liked them and didn't want to leave their home, but she swallowed her emotions as she sat on her bed waiting for them to come in.

When James and Ashley entered the room, Rebecca was surprised to see wetness around their eyes. Clearly they had been crying. They pulled up chairs and sat quietly for a minute. Finally, Ashley choked out, "Rebecca." James continued, "This changes nothing. You are part of this family. That's it." Ashley and James exchanged glances, then got up and hugged Rebecca and left the room. Rebecca sat stunned, tears streaming down her cheeks. The next morning, for the first time in a long time, Rebecca joined the rest of the family for breakfast before school.

Processing

1. How has full love (or lack thereof) affected Rebecca's life before moving in with Ashley and James?
2. How did Ashley and James demonstrate full love to Rebecca? Which aspect of full love do you think had the greatest impact on Rebecca?
3. How does Ashley's and James's expression of full love for Rebecca help her experience life as fair or just?
4. How might Ashley's and James's expression of full love for Rebecca affect their ability to be vulnerable and intimate with one another?
5. Does love really conquer all? What types of issues are Ashley, James, and Rebecca still going to have to work through together?

References

Brown, B. (2012). *Daring greatly: How the courage to be vulnerable transforms the way we live, love, parent, and lead*. New York: Gotham Books.

Canary, D. J., & Stafford, L. (1992). Relational maintenance strategies and equity in marriage. *Communication Monographs, 59*, 243–267.

Chapman, E. N., & Werner-Wilson, R. J. (2008). Does positive youth development predict adolescent attitudes about sexuality? *Adolescence, 43*, 505–523.

Chapman, G. D. (1992). *The five love languages: The secret to love that lasts*. Chicago: Northfield Publishing.

Cheney, G., Christensen, L. T., & Dailey, S. L. (2014). Communicating identity and identification in and around organizations. In L. L. Putnam & D. K. Mumby (Eds.), *The Sage handbook of organizational communication: Advances in theory, research, and methods* (pp. 695–716). Los Angeles: Sage.

Hendrick, S. S., & Hendrick, C. (1992). *Romantic love*. Beverly Hills, CA: Sage.

Kelley, D. L. (2012). *Marital communication*. Cambridge, UK: Polity.

Lewis, C. S. (1946). *The great divorce*. New York: Harper Collins.

Noller, P. (1996). What is this thing called love? Defining the love that supports marriage and family. *Personal Relationships, 3*, 97–115.

Petronio, S. (2002). *Boundaries of privacy: Dialectics of disclosure.* Albany, NY: State University of New York Press.

Simon, P. (1965). I am a rock. In *The Paul Simon songbook.* New York: Columbia Records.

Stanley, S. M., Whitton, S. W., Sadberry, S. L., Clements, M. L., & Markman, H. J. (2006). Sacrifice as a predictor of marital outcomes. *Family Process, 45,* 289–303.

Sternberg, R. J. (1986). A triangular theory of love. *Psychological Review, 93,* 119–135.

Sternberg, R. J. (1997). Construct validation of a triangular love scale. *European Journal of Social Psychology, 27,* 313–335.

Tutu, D. M. (1999). *No future without forgiveness.* New York: Random House.

Van Wel, F. (1994). "I count my parents among my best friends": Youths bonds with parents and friends in the Netherlands. *Journal of Marriage and the Family, 56,* 835–843.

Waldron, V. R., & Kelley, D. L. (2008). *Communicating forgiveness.* Thousand Oaks, CA: Sage.

5

INTERPERSONAL ADVOCACY

Creating Spaces

Advocacy is a term that has been associated with speaking up for people-groups and the causes most salient to those groups. When we think of advocacy, we often picture Dr. Martin Luther King Jr. on the steps of the Lincoln Memorial, his voice forever etched in our memories as the voice of change. We may also think of lawyers who advocate for their clients, and lobbyists who advocate for their interest groups. Or you may think of advocacy as related to an under-represented group that you belong to. For example, the self-described "Leading Gay News Source" is called *The Advocate* (Jan 27, 2015, http://heremediamagazines.com/pride8_offer.php). And, while these uses of the term are certainly appropriate, the perspective offered in this chapter reframes this concept into our personal relationships. Parents, siblings, friends, and romantic partners are all advocates when they are in just, loving relationships. For our purposes, interpersonal advocacy is the *process of creating spaces where if something good can happen, it will.*

Approaches to Advocacy

Advocacy takes many forms, but one central distinction between approaches guides our understanding of advocacy as creating spaces—certain approaches to advocacy focus on *speaking for others*, while alternate approaches focus on helping others *find their own voice*. The United States legal system is representative of the first advocacy approach. A lawyer represents a client *against* a plaintiff or defendant. Often, the two conflicting parties have little or no direct interaction with one another, and may not even speak directly to the judge. The lawyer advocates by speaking *for* her client. On the other hand, a mentor represents the second approach as he helps his mentee find his own voice. The mentor works to create a safe space (physically and psychologically) for the mentee to learn and grow, and eventually stand and speak for himself.

Falk and Adeline (1995) write about advocacy within the field of nursing and make distinctions that are relevant to us here. Their work is particularly pertinent because nurses are *care providers*—not a bad way to think about interpersonal advocacy. Falk and Adeline distinguish between types of advocacy. Simplistic advocacy and paternalistic advocacy are approaches wherein the advocate speaks *for* others. Simplistic advocacy is when one pleads a cause for or acts on behalf of another. Paternalistic advocacy is similar in that the advocate acts *for* another person but, in this case, without the consent of the person needing help, presumably because it is for that person's own good. *Speaking for* others, as a form of advocacy, is necessary, at times, particularly when time is of the essence or the person being advocated for does not have the ability to speak for herself. For instance, when a quick response is needed to avoid hurt, danger, or damage, then we should speak up for those who have no voice or have no space from which to speak. Or, as in the case of a parent, paternalistic advocacy may be necessary because a young child lacks the maturity to make his own decisions. Yet, at some point, we must help the other person discover his own voice (the point of good parenting, yes?). If we fail to do this, we eventually destroy the other person's right to self-determination, and put ourselves in a position where we carry too much responsibility for others.

A stunning example of how *speaking for* can be used to help others *find their own voice* comes from lawyer Kimberly Motley. One of the many things that Kimberly does is advocate for the rights of Afghan women, using Afghan law. A landmark case of hers was representing Sahar, an Afghan woman forced into marriage at age 12, before the Afghan Supreme Court. Motley won the case for this young woman, but in the process something else wonderful happened. As Kimberly states it, "So there we were at the Supreme Court arguing in front of 12 Afghan justices, me as an American female lawyer, and Sahar, a young woman who when I met her couldn't speak above a whisper. She stood up, she found her voice, and my girl told them that she wanted justice, and she got it" (Motley, 2014). A powerful story, but notice the progression—Kimberly speaks for Sahar as her representative, and then . . . Sahar stands and finds her own voice!

The shift from speaking *for others* to creating spaces where others can find and use *their own voice* is a significant one. Advocates who operate from this perspective are more common than might be imagined. Think of good mentors, parents, friends, and romantic partners who help us become whole, embracing our full humanity. Once again, Falk and Adeline (1995) aid us here. They discuss existential and human advocacy as approaches that aid others in finding meaning in their personal experience and, in so doing, shore up the integrity of the person. This often means participating with and encouraging others to reevaluate needs and clarify values. For example, this last week I talked, separately, with two of our graduate students who were trying to understand the suffering and angst they have endured in their graduate studies. Besides affirming their emotional experience, I encouraged them to find deeper meaning in their struggle and to use it as a time to better understand themselves: What is it they enjoy? What do they struggle with? What are they good at? Why do they enjoy or struggle with these things? I didn't have advice for them regarding decisions they were trying to make. But I did have the ability to help them explore their own human experience.

Desiring for others to each find their own voice is consistent with our previous discussions emphasizing the essential need to understand what is *fair* and what is *good* for others and ourselves. Our "fair" and "good" understanding must not result from unilateral, paternalistic thinking, but rather emerge through ongoing dialogue and being with others. As Tutu (1999) teaches regarding Ubuntu, we exist because of others.

Interpersonal Advocacy as Creating Spaces

In the hopes of helping us all find our own voices, I use the phrase, *creating spaces,* to conceptualize interpersonal advocacy. Creating spaces is undergirded by a central assumption—you cannot control people to such an extent that they consistently act or believe how you prefer. In other words, as an advocate, you can participate in creating a relational space for growth, but the other person has to be willing and able to enter that space and, eventually, co-create that space so that she is able to think and act in a manner true to her own self. One way to think about this is—whenever possible, *create spaces where if something good can happen, it will.* A personal story with one of my sons illustrates this central principle. Daniel dropped out of high school in his junior year, while I was teaching Family Communication at Arizona State University! Oh, the irony. One afternoon, during this difficult time, Daniel looked at me and said, "Dad, you can't make me change. I have to want to change." Such wisdom from a 17-year-old. He was absolutely right. All Ann (my wife) and I could do was try to *create a space where if something good can happen, it will* so that when Daniel was ready, something good would happen—and, it eventually did.

It is important to recognize that while Ann and I did what we could to create a relationally safe space for Daniel, this space was ultimately co-created by Daniel *and* ourselves. All relationship spaces are co-created. No one person can unilaterally determine the nature of a relationship. Edna Rogers (2008) describes this process: "Relationships can be viewed as evolving 'art forms' creatively performed by the participants in the ongoing movement of their communicative 'dance'" (p. 336). Similarly, Baxter, Norwood, and Nebel (2012) describe Bakhtin's (1993) notion of aesthetic love as "a way of co-enacting a kind of joint Being with another" (p. 24). Conceptualizing our relationships as jointly created spaces safeguards us from falling into unhealthy paternalistic patterns and moves us toward experiencing the beauty of one another and of the relationship itself.

What does *a place where if something good can happen, it will,* look like? It looks like a space where relational partners are freely discovering and expressing *each one's own voice.* Later, in Chapter Eight: "Saving Face," I discuss issues of face and identity, but suffice it to say that before you can speak your own voice, you have to discover your own voice. A theme that has run through the first four chapters of this book emphasizes that just, moral, loving relationships are relationships where partners help one another discover their full selves, their joint humanity. Again, Edna Rogers (2008) reinforces this perspective by conceptualizing "communication as a social process, the life giving essence of our humanness" (p. 340), and Baxter et al. (2012) describe Bakhtin's aesthetic love as a "profoundly creative act in which Other is constituted" (p. 25), wherein our "self" grows through interaction with others.

Advocacy as creating spaces is also characterized by people speaking their own voices. This is central to dialogue. As we discussed in Chapter Three: "Good Relationships," dialogue involves a process of finding one's own self and sharing that self with appropriate others. But, even more so, Baxter (2004) contends that when in dialogue, "Parties owe each other the opportunity for their selves to become" (p. 118). Interestingly, early work looking at interpersonal justice framed justice as "voice" (Hill, Exline, & Cohen, 2005). *Just relationships are relationships where both partners are truly free to give voice to their thoughts and inner experience.* In this vein, mentoring relationships can be viewed as interpersonal advocacy when both participants benefit from the relationship and mentees "develop their own strategies for coping" (Philip & Hendry, 2000, p. 213).

A hallmark of *advocacy as creating spaces* is that relational partners join one another in a context that is *safe*. Advocacy as creating spaces involves crafting safe places for relational partners to co-exist. Mead and MacNeil (2006) in their work related to peer support, argue that safety has come to simply mean risk assessment and soothing someone's discomfort, strategies which can fail to take into account the emotional and power-oriented dynamics of relational safety. Instead, they suggest that safety happens in the context of mutually responsible, trusting relationships, where we don't judge or make assumptions about one other. Full love (as discussed in Chapter Four: "Love Relationships") creates this safe environment. Characterized by healthy self-sacrifice, mature relational partners care for one another, speak up for one another when it is needed, and use this "speaking up" to eventually open a space for the partner to find and speak her own voice. In essence, our partner's good will and actions creates a space where it is safe for us to get on our feet and act for ourselves.

Self-Advocacy

To this point, we have embraced advocacy as a process of jointly creating spaces where relational partners find their own voices and speak. Deeply embedded in this process is learning to advocate for oneself. As we have discussed, together we endeavor to *create spaces where if something good can happen, it will,* but each partner, individually, has to choose to enter and remain in those spaces. In this sense, each person becomes his or her own advocate. Foundationally, each of us is able to make decisions that help us find our own voices and move toward a fuller understanding of our own humanity.

Self-advocacy follows a similar pattern as other-oriented advocacy, except that we are creating spaces for our own selves. In essence, self-advocacy is a process of giving oneself permission to find one's own voice and then, speak, to become known. Manusov (2015) encourages us to practice mindfulness as a moral way of being that creates a space where we are "fully with another person and ourselves *just as we are*" (Manusov, 2015; see Chapter Three: "Good Relationships"). That is, a central part of mindfulness is being present with oneself (discovery of our inner self) holding a nonjudgmental mindset (acceptance of self). Greenland (2010) suggests that we teach our children self-compassion, by encouraging them in the following way: "rest in your [internal] safe place knowing that you are complete and whole just the way you are" (p. 123). Mindfulness helps us advocate for ourselves as we create an internal space *where if something good can happen, it will.* In this sense, mindfulness creates a foundation that enables each of us to find our own voice in the presence of others.

FELONY

by Shanae G.*

I just want a second chance at life
Single mother forced to live off welfare
No one wants to hire me
It was just a one misfortune
I committed a felony
A non-dangerous non-*Repetitive* one
Now look at my life
They say they don't want you to fuck up
But the truth is how could you not
Hell u can't get a job worth saving ur life
And they expect you to do right
But I will not stop at trying to be a better me
Forget what you think
I will succeed
So please stop doubting me and just have faith in me
I don't need your worries added on to mine
Just allow me this opportunity
You might be able to help me instead of hinder me
But before you tell me one more time
How going to school is not an option for me
And that I will never be anything and just keep
Describing how I may be wasting my time
BUT how about this just
Unfold me before you judge me
and just give me a second chance at what i call life.

Shanae's own commentary

People are always judging people who have made mistakes or are continuously making mistakes but no one is listening, no one is helping you build a better life. When you can't obtain a job you just go back to what you know. When you don't have a stress releaser, you lose it. When no one wants to give you another chance you die inside so please stop judging everyone who makes a mistake. I want to help bring alive change and keep focused, but provide hope.

*Shanae is a student I met through my Inner-City Families class.

Building Advocacy-Based Relationships

Advocacy is a relational perspective based on creating spaces with our relational partners, in order to find and give voice to our true selves. To facilitate the seeing and doing of advocacy in our personal relationships, I now draw upon insights from literature on peer support and youth mentoring. I finish with thoughts on mindfulness and play as advocacy.

Advocacy as Mutuality

Creating a space where if something good can happen, it will is a process of co-creation, of mutuality. Sherry Mead's organization, *Intentional Peer Support*, provides an example of this process. Based on her own encounters with the mental health system, Mead was prompted to found an organization with the goal of helping others find wholeness through dialogue and mutuality in relationships. To this aim, she proposes four peer support tasks (2014). First, the core of peer support is *connection*. Connection happens in the moment when you realize that someone else finally "gets it" and doesn't judge you for who you are. The second task, *worldview*, is taking time to understand how we've come to see the world as we do, how we've come to know what we know. The potential result of this is self- and other-compassion as we better realize the influences that have shaped our life experience. And, as important, we gain perspective that our worldview is not the only way to see things (more on this in Chapter Six: "Worldview: Your Relationship Frame"). *Mutuality*, the third task, is characterized by equality and reciprocity. This pivotal task frees us from constant self-focus and the dangers of embracing the roles of victim or hero. Seeing myself as victim keeps me embedded in a worldview that says I have no choice or control over my life. On the other hand, engaging in my own self-hero-worship, as a mentor, blinds me to the fact that others' transformation is primarily due to their own choices and that I have my own need for transformation. In short, in the spirit of Ubuntu (see Chapter Four: "Love Relationships") it is only in mutuality that we come to see our humanity. The fourth task, *moving toward*, reorients growth and transformation toward the future (what we hope and desire), as opposed to running from the past. Instead of dwelling on past problems, this perspective encourages us to think about the type of future we hope for and take action.

> *Living It Out: Do you "get" your relationship partner? Do they "get" you? What can you do to facilitate more understanding of one another?*
>
> *Living It Out: Individually, take time for you and your partner to think about your own worldviews—how have you come to think about and experience the world as you have? Now share with one another. (Hold on to these as we will come back to this in Chapter Six.)*
>
> *Living It Out: To what extent would you describe your relationship as mutual? How often do you sense equality and reciprocity in your relationship?*

Living It Out: What would it look like for you to look forward (What do I want for me, personally, and for our relationship?) instead of ruminating about the past (What haven't I liked?)? As a friend and colleague of mine suggests, How might we harvest memories from the past to shape a just future?

Advocacy as Shared Experience

Classic mentoring is a relationship between experienced and less-experienced persons. This is often an adult-youth relationship or a work relationship between senior and "rookie" employees. Liang and Rhodes (2007) describe mentoring as an enduring relationship with lasting benefits. I've adapted their perennial gardening/mentoring analogy into five mentoring tasks. First, prepare. No one intentionally buys a new plant and leaves it in the container in the garage. We have in mind a place where the plant will fit in terms of the aesthetics of our home, and appropriate soil and weather conditions. Likewise, we are looking for some type of "fit" between mentor and mentee. Not everyone does well with inner-city youth or is cut out to work with addicts. It is important to realize that fit does *not* mean that mentor and mentee have to come from similar backgrounds, however there must be some foundation that suggests they will be able to hear one another. This may mean some background work by the mentor. And, the mentor should do a self-check to make certain he has the skills to listen and affirm someone who likely has substantive differences from himself—in other words, he has to believe that he has what it takes to create the climate for new growth. Second, plant. Putting a new plant in the ground requires special care—plenty of water, fertilizer, and protection from the elements. The early days of the mentoring relationship are characterized by a lot of positive effort (e.g., time spent together, joint activities) to get the roots to take hold. This stage is critical to the success of this pairing. Third, weed. Good growth conditions can lead to a proliferation of weeds, along with perennial plant growth. When doing well in a mentoring relationship, some mentees experience pressure from their social network to stop changing—"We want *you* back again, the way we knew you!" Fourth, grow deep. Many plants experience quick growth in the beginning, but the trick is to get the roots to grow deep. This often means deep watering, fertilizing, pruning, and protecting and mending during storms. In other words, as the relationship matures there will be deep talks, moving toward understanding, working through a lot of "crap," and dealing with conflict. These are normal processes that create a solid root system for the relationship. Fifth, adapt. Be sure to stay open to change in the relationship as the seasons change. For example, one wants to be cautious of pruning during the new growth of early spring, yet, failing to prune before the storms of summer can lead to long-term damage. A critical aspect, that builds throughout these five mentoring steps, is a strong emotional bond between mentor and mentee (Wilson & Gettings, 2012). This emotional bond facilitates a sense of mutual trust, creating a safe environment for change.

Living It Out: If you are mentoring someone less experienced than yourself, go through the five gardening/mentoring tasks (this could be parent-child, mentor in a community organization, senior employee-rookie, or friends helping each other). Identify where you are in the process. Ask hard questions: "Have I prepared?" "Is this a good 'fit' for me?" "Am I 'watering' this process?" "Am I weeding and pruning when necessary?" "Are we going deep?" "Am I adaptable enough?"

Advocacy as Mindfulness

As we discussed previously, mindfulness is a moral means of being with ourselves and others. When we are mindfully present with others we are aware without judgment (based on Manusov, 2015), creating a safe space *where if something good can happen, it will.* Thich Nhat Hanh (1991) echoes these thoughts, "Understanding and love are not two things, but just one. . . . when you love, you naturally act in a way that can relieve the suffering of people" (p. 79–80). Consider this perspective in light of self- and other-advocacy. When I feel emotionally and physically safe with you (not judged, but understood), I am free to observe and change. You have become an advocate for me by simply being with me and not judging. And, when I take time for self-awareness without judgment, I am truly free to change for the "good." I have become my own advocate.

Living It Out: What if you began to accept yourself for who you are? What might you be free to see in yourself, and how might your life change for the good?

Living It Out: If you are a mentor with someone, how might being "present without judgment" give the other person the freedom to change for the good?

Living It Out: This week try hugging meditation (as described by Thich Nhat Hanh, 1991). When you hug someone 'hello' or 'goodbye' (or just because you need a hug!), deeply breathe in and out three times. Somewhere during the second breath you will begin to feel present, connected, to the other person. For me, I start to feel safe.

Advocacy as Play

I love to play. One reason is that typically when I'm playing, I'm mindful. I'm present. I'm in the moment. In an article on advocacy and children, Powell (2004) reminds us that "young people can be open and trusting and gregarious and want to be held and to play" (p. 3). Play values the other unconditionally. Play connects us together. Famed anthropologist Ashley Montagu (1989), reminds us that play is a process of "re-creation" (p. 130). In this sense, play is one way of *creating a space where if something good can happen, it will.* Montagu goes on to claim: "Play has probably been the most important factor in the evolution of social behavior among vertebrates and . . . of the mental and spiritual life of mankind" (p. 131).

Since *advocacy as play* may have caught you by surprise, let me offer a few possibilities as to how to think about it. First, play is more a mindset, than something you do. You can play games in a way that is not play at all, and you can make work play when it is spontaneous and creative. Author Madeleine L'Engle (1980) puts it wonderfully, "Drudgery is not what work is meant to be. Our work should be our play. If we watch a child at play for a few minutes, 'seriously' at play, we see that all his energies are concentrated on it. He is working very hard on it. And that is how the artist works . . ." (p. 167). The work of advocacy becomes play as we dance with our relational partners (Rogers, 2008) creating a work of relationship art (the name of my personal website). Second, play drops certain inhibitions and, as such, gives us increased access to one another. Jimmy Fallon has transformed the *Tonight Show* in part by playing games with his guests. Through playing games you get to see a part of celebrities that you might never see during a standard interview. Finally, play connects us as we are free to be ourselves. I asked a single friend of mine, in her mid-thirties, what she was looking for in a man. She quickly responded, "Someone I can be silly with." Someone she can play with. Someone with whom she can be herself.

Since I was 16 years old I have been involved with an organization called *Young Life*. *Young Life* is a faith-based organization that works with middle-school students to adults, preadolescents who haven't gone through puberty to adolescents who are pregnant, kids from generational poverty to kids who have considerable wealth. A hallmark of what they do is play with people in order to gently disarm their defense mechanisms. Adult couples who haven't had a real conversation in weeks suddenly find themselves squeezing through an innertube together. Gang members used to posturing and protecting image find themselves submerged in a creek, when they can't swim! Teen moms who have placed their trust only in their child, suddenly find themselves laughing uncontrollably with an adult mentor as they are dropped 40 feet on a swing that is part of one of *Young Life*'s ropes courses. Perspective change. Dropped inhibitions. Connection. Play is serious business!

> *Living It Out: How might you introduce play into your life today, or the life of someone you care for? Is there a way to have a fresh 'playful' perspective about something you're already doing?*
>
> *Living It Out: How can you allow play to "re-create" your inner self or the self of your partner? Is there a way that play can drop your inhibitions enough that you are open to change?*
>
> *Living It Out: Can you do something playful with someone you know to create more connection between the two of you? Can play create a safe space where if something good can happen, it will?*

Case 5.1

Brenda and her son, Tyler, age 27, live together in a two-bedroom apartment. After losing his job, Tyler lost all confidence in himself. In fact, even when offered a chance to apply for a job in a company where a friend worked, Tyler let the opportunity pass—"I'm not qualified for that. This process is impossible. No one wants someone who has been fired." However, Brenda sent Tyler's resume to their friend and within two days Tyler was scheduled for a job interview. That afternoon, the conversation went something like this:

Brenda: Exciting that you got the interview! (*said with a bit too much enthusiasm*)

Tyler: I guess.

Brenda: Look, I know this is hard, but you have to snap out of this funk.

Tyler: Why? So you feel happier and I can eventually move out?

Brenda: Ok, wait. Do you think this is about me?

Tyler: Isn't it always when you're trying to "help" me? I know you want me to move out so you can turn my room into an office.

Brenda: (*takes a deep breath*) Let's start over. Tyler, maybe it doesn't always feel like it, but I really love you, and I just hate seeing you down on yourself. You have so much to offer that company. And . . . you have so much to offer me.

Tyler: I hear your words, but they just don't mean anything to me right now.

Brenda: I get that. I mean I really do. Do you think that watching your dad change careers so many times, and never really "make it," has left some fear inside you?

Tyler: Maybe. I can't help but think of the times I would come home from school with him just sitting on the couch watching TV. Your "helping" reminds me of the times you would "encourage" Dad to try again. I know I'm just like him. It all looks like failure to me.

Brenda: Wow. I needed to hear that. I know that I can be controlling, at times, when I try to help others. I don't want to control you. And, I certainly don't think you're "just like your dad!" Can you tell me how I can know when you want help, and how to better help you without seeming controlling?

Tyler: I don't know. It all still seems so overwhelming at times.

Brenda: I tell you what. I have a gift card for Tomassi's. What if we talk about this more over a nice dinner?

Tyler: I could get into that.

Brenda: Perfect! I can be ready in 20!

Processing

1. How were Brenda and Tyler creating a space *where if something good can happen, it will*?

2. Think back to the four peer support tasks. How well did (or, will) Brenda and Tyler find connection, explore worldview, and look forward? Was there a sense of mutuality to their discussion?

3. Do you think mindfulness was a factor in this interaction? How do you think mindfulness might help Brenda and Tyler in the future?

4. To what extent is play used as advocacy in this scenario?

Case 5.2

Cynthia attends a large, upper-middle class church in Chicago. She is white, comfortable financially, has two children (who she had when she was 25 and 27), and has been married for 20 years. She was emotionally moved by a speaker she heard at a volunteerism workshop and, shortly after, contacted Young Moms to volunteer as a mentor with a teen mother. After going through a small amount of training and background checks, Cynthia was assigned to Paige. Their once-a-week meetings were constructed around an activity for moms and mentors to interact with one another, followed by a teaching time focused on a parenting topic, and ended with group discussion.

The first night that Cynthia met Paige, Cynthia was surprised at Paige's seeming disinterest. Even though Cynthia was aware that it would take time to establish a relationship, she hadn't expected to feel so uncomfortable. Paige was polite, but conversation dragged as she gave brief answers to all of Cynthia's questions. At a loss for what to do, Cynthia actually left earlier than she had planned. Over the next week Cynthia thought about quitting, "Maybe I've made a mistake. Maybe this isn't really for me." But she returned for week two.

The next few weeks took on a friendlier tone. During the mentor/mom activities Paige occasionally shared more personally and Cynthia discussed some of her own experience as a mother, as well. However, starting in week six, Paige began sharing some information that made Cynthia uncomfortable. One week Paige was short on rent money because she had spent a large sum on alcohol and food for a weekend-long party at her house. Cynthia felt like she and Paige had a good talk about the situation and that Paige understood that she couldn't spend money like that and needed to put her children first. But, then, two weeks later Paige confessed having spent a large sum of money so she and her boyfriend could go to Las Vegas . . . now, she didn't have enough money for her children's upcoming after-school sports camp. Cynthia took this very personally. She couldn't understand how Paige could make such a decision, especially after their talk two weeks previous. Feeling overwhelmed and hopeless by the situation, Cynthia wrote a letter to the head of Young Moms expressing her frustration with their program and resigned as a volunteer.

Processing

1. Apply the perennial analogy to Cynthia and Paige's mentoring experience. Do you think Cynthia was properly prepared? Was planting and weeding done well? Was growing deep and adapting part of this mentoring relationship? If so, how?
2. What sense of mutuality or emotional bond was evident in this relationship?
3. Did Cynthia and Paige *create a space where if something good could happen, it would*?
4. How could mindfulness or play have helped this mentoring relationship?

References

The Advocate (2015, Jan 27). http://heremediamagazines.com/pride8_offer.php

Bakhtin, M. M. (1993). *Toward a philosophy of the act* (V. Liapunov, Ed.; M. Holquist, Trans.). Austin: University of Texas Press. (Original work published in 1986).

Baxter, L. A. (2004). Dialogues of relating. In R. Anderson, L. A. Baxter, & K. N. Cissna (Eds.), *Dialogue: Theorizing difference in communication studies* (pp. 107–124). Thousand Oaks, CA: Sage.

Baxter, L. A., Norwood, K. M., & Nebel, S. (2012). Aesthetic relating. In T. J. Socha & M. J. Pitts (Eds.), *The positive side of interpersonal communication* (pp. 19–38). New York: Peter Lang.

Falk, R., & Adeline, R. (1995). Advocacy and empowerment: Dichotomous or synchronous concepts? *Advances in Nursing Science, 18*(2), 25–32.

Greenland, S. J. (2010). *The mindful child.* New York: Atria Paperback.

Hanh, T. N. (1991). *Peace is every step: The path of mindfulness in everyday life.* New York: Bantam Books.

Hill, P. C., Exline, J. J., & Cohen, A. B. (2005). The social psychology of justice and forgiveness in civil and organizational settings. In E. Worthington, Jr. (Ed.), *Handbook of forgiveness* (pp. 477–490). New York: Routledge.

L'Engle, M. (1980). *Walking on water: Reflections on faith and art.* Wheaton, IL: Harold Shaw Publishers.

Liang, B., & Rhodes, J. (2007). Guest editorial: Cultivating the vital element of youth mentoring. *Applied Development Science, 11*, 104–107.

Manusov, V. (2015). Mindfulness as morality: Awareness, nonjudgment, and nonreactivity in couples' communication. In V. R. Waldron & D. L. Kelley (Eds.), *Moral talk across the lifespan* (pp. 183–201). New York: Peter Lang.

Mead, S. (2014). http://www.intentionalpeersupport.org/wp-content/uploads/2014/12/IPS-An-Alternative-Approach-2014-First-Chapter.pdf

Mead, S., & MacNeil, C. (2006). Peer support: What makes it unique? *International Journal of Psychosocial Rehabilitation, 10*, 29–37.

Montagu, A. (1989). *Growing young.* Westport, CT: Bergin & Garvey.

Motley, K. (2014). How I defend the rule of law. http://www.ted.com/talks/kimberley_motley_how_i_defend_the_rule_of_law

Philip, K., & Hendry, L. B. (2000). Making sense of mentoring or mentoring making sense? Reflections on the mentoring process by adult mentors with young people. *Journal of Community and Applied Social Psychology, 10*, 211–223.

Powell, W. E. (2004). The play is the thing: From the interpersonal to advocacy. *The Journal of Contemporary Social Services, 85*, 3–4.

Rogers, L. E. (2008). Relational communication theory. In L. A. Baxter & D. O. Braithwaite (Eds.), *Engaging theories in interpersonal communication* (pp. 335–347). Los Angeles: Sage.

Socha, T. J., & Pitts, M. J. (2012). Positive interpersonal communication as child's play. In T. J. Socha & M. J. Pitts (Eds.), *The positive side of interpersonal communication* (pp. 323–324). New York: Peter Lang.

Tutu, D. M. (1999). *No future without forgiveness.* New York: Random House.

Wilson, S. R., & Gettings, P. E. (2012). Nurturing children as assets: A positive approach to preventing child maltreatment and promoting healthy youth development. In T. J. Socha & M. J. Pitts (Eds.), *The positive sided of interpersonal communication* (pp. 277–295). New York: Peter Lang.

PART II
Barriers to Just Relationships
Perceptions That Separate

6

WORLDVIEW

Your Relationship Frame

As an amateur photographer, I have learned that "framing" a shot affects *how* I see *what* I see. I am friends with a few professional photographers on Instagram. I have learned from them how an average picture can be made extraordinary, simply by changing the perspective on a particular point of interest. For example, on a mountain trail near my home, there is a tree that hikers decorate for Christmas. I have taken numerous pictures of this tree, but they all have seemed average. Somehow I couldn't capture on a screen what I experienced in real life. Then, two days ago, I saw a friend's post of a decorated tree alongside a trail. He chose to focus on one red ribbon, leaving an expansive panorama in the background. His picture captured what I had been feeling during my multiple attempts to portray the essence of our own trail tree. Learning to frame a shot, noticing subtle variances in the light, and balancing the picture's composition with objects foreground and background and on the horizontal plane, can make all the difference in what one sees.

We all have frames through which we view the world and, specifically, our relationships to others. For a moment, think about holding an 8 x 10 frame in front of your face. Hold it vertically. Now horizontally or, maybe, diagonally. How does this influence what you see? Those of you who wear glasses know what I'm talking about. I have a pair of glasses with no lenses in them that look very "academic-like" that I sometimes wear on test days. But they so alter my vision that, even with no lenses, I can only bear to wear them for part of the class period. My point is that *how* we frame what we see affects *what* we see.

Our relationship frames (relationship worldview) are created and maintained through personal experiences and culture and subculture. For example, an African American student of mine recently gave a presentation describing the experience of an African American gay male. Based on an in-depth interview, he described the diverse perspectives, or relationship frames, that were held by various constituents in this man's life (family, partner, self). The tendency was for each person to view the situation from one perspective, one frame. For example, his mother saw his sexual orientation from the following relationship frame: "African American men are not gay," "Christian men are not gay." Although the person being interviewed had once held these same perspectives, at one point in his life he chose to switch frames entirely: "I don't identify with my African American heritage," "I am no longer Christian." However, later in life he chose to return to his original relationship frames, but use them to view the situation from a different vantage point: "African American men vary in their sexual expression and orientation," "As a Christian, love is my highest value."

When we learn to frame what we see from different vantage points, we create spaces for social justice and advocacy for one another. When we use a single frame and refuse to explore alternative perspectives, this narrow and rigid approach inhibits social justice. Restricted approaches become self-serving over time and limit one's ability to care for others. Broad relationship perspectives create a vision of life where *if something good can happen, it will* (see Chapter Five: "Interpersonal Advocacy: Creating Spaces"). Narrow approaches to understanding others define "good" simply from what seems clear from one limited viewpoint. Broad relationship approaches promote dialogue to gain new perspective.

When relationship frames are stuck on one perspective they fail to provide a clear view of the world in which we live—they only see things from one angle, are distorted by glaring or nonexistent light, and allow for erroneous objects to steal the focus of the image. When we have broad relationship frames that provide a variety of perspectives, we get a clearer view of the world. Our relationship challenge is to create shared relationship frames from which to establish just and loving relationships. We achieve this through dialogue as we co-create "frames and lenses to view, value, and legitimate our experience" (Haste & Abrahams, 2008, p. 382) and the experience of those for whom we care.

Understanding Your Relationship Frame

Worldview is the set of beliefs and assumptions that describes our perspective or experience of reality (Rivera-Koltko, 2004). These beliefs and assumptions take into account how we understand the nature of what it means to be human, the potential for human change, our ability as human beings to remember the past and imagine the future, the nature of our goal-orientation as human beings, perspectives on self and other, and our relationship orientation (Kluckhohn, 1950; Rivera-Koltko, 2004). How we view these elements determines how we perceive other persons in our world. In essence, they create what I have been calling a *relationship frame* (Solomon & McLaren, 2008).

Your relationship frame is your relationship worldview. Remember from Chapter Five: "Interpersonal Advocacy: Creating Spaces," Sherry Mead suggests that peer support involves understanding one's own and one's partner's worldviews (Mead, 2014). Understanding your relationship frame is essential because your relationship worldview influences how you label and categorize your relationships and relationship partners, establishes what those labels and categories mean to you, and determines how you will react or respond to your relationship experience.

You can think of it this way. A primary task we have as human beings is determining what things "count as," and specifically for this discussion, what they count as relationally. As children we learn what counts as what—that is Mom, this is Dad; that is a cat, this is a dog. As we grow and develop, the categories become more complex—that is feminine, this is masculine; that is control, this is love. Eventually, we determine what we think counts as good or bad, or just or unjust (see Chapter Two: "Just Relationships" and Chapter Three: "Good Relationships" for more on this). Determining what things count as, relationally, largely depends on the relationship frame we are looking through. However, we are mostly unaware of this process. We frequently assume that what counts as good to me, *is* good, or *should* be counted as good for everyone. This is one of the fundamental elements that create relational conflict—"I thought we agreed we would keep the kitchen clean?" "We did. And, I put all the dishes in the sink before I left." As such, a fundamental goal in our relationships is to understand for ourselves, and our partners, what counts as what.

In the following pages, I overview three theories that help us understand how we create relationship frames through which to view our relational worlds: relational framing theory, attachment theory, and attribution theory.

Relational Framing Theory

Relational Framing Theory proposes that individuals view "dominance-submissiveness and affiliation-disaffiliation as functional frames that help people process social messages, resolve ambiguities, and draw relational inferences" (Solomon & McLaren, 2008, p. 104). Or, to return to my photography analogy, when relational partners interact they view behaviors through a relational frame that sets the scene in such a way that they see it as indicating control and submission or as related to connection and distance. For instance, if my wife and I are using different relational frames, my "affiliative," connecting behavior could be viewed by her as controlling. More specifically, my "helping her do things the 'right' way" could be viewed by her as always "telling her what to do."

Once we begin to see things as indicating control-submission or connection-distance, attention is directed to behaviors in any given interaction that confirm this perspective, intensify it, or draw it into question. For instance, once I begin to see behaviors from a dominance perspective, I begin to find cues that confirm or disconfirm that idea. Something as simple as you standing and raising your voice while I'm sitting could confirm for me that the dominance relational frame is the correct way to view this interaction ("You are trying to control me," "You think you're the boss in this relationship," "You always get your way"). Alternatively, if you continue to exhibit those behaviors, but include animated storytelling and asking for my perspective, I might like the fact that you are sharing with me, and change my relational frame to one of connection ("You are a team player," "You like to connect with others by being expressive").

The framing process inhibits building socially just relationships when the relational frames we use keep us stuck in one perspective (I can only see you as wanting to control me). As we have discussed thus far, social justice is dependent on a process of co-creation that requires adaptation to one another and agreed-upon relational frames. Unfortunately, changing your worldview, or relational frame, comes at significant cost. Changing how we view others typically requires extensive alterations in terms of how we respond to them. These changes may be seen as taking too much time or energy. Or, we might think that if we change one way that we see things, the change will never stop! In fact, research has demonstrated that people will go to great lengths not to change their worldview or relationship frame. For example, Bulman-Janoff (1989) has done interesting work that suggests a person, at times, will go so far as to take the blame for a negative event rather than alter his worldview. The bottom line is change and understanding are difficult and require great effort. (I further address this issue in the section, *Changing One's Relational Frame.*)

Attachment Theory

Attachment theory provides another perspective as to how relationship frames are created and affect our perceptions. Attachment theory proposes that individuals develop mental relational models (relational frames) based on infants' attachments to their primary caregivers, although these mental models can also be affected by other relational experiences (Feeney, 2005, 2009; Trees, 2006). Significantly, it is believed that these early attachments influence future relationships. For example, someone who had consistent care and love from her mother will likely be more secure in her adult romantic relationships.

A key element of understanding this process is that our mental models provide relational frames that orient our perspective as to whether we are loveworthy, and whether our relational partners are trustworthy, available, and responsive when needed (Feeney, 2005, 2009). This relational perspective influences our willingness and ability to build just relationships with others based on equity and respect (e.g., it is hard to be open with someone that you don't trust"). In addition, if our relational frame reflects an image of our own self that is not loveworthy, we are severely compromised in our ability to self-advocate and even serve as an equal relational partner.

Attachment theorists also show us how individuals' attachment styles (mental relationship models) are enacted in various ways (Hazan & Shaver, 1987; Trees, 2006). *Avoidant* individuals fear intimacy and are reticent to depend on others. Overall, they have difficulty accepting their partners. *Anxious-ambivalent* individuals experience a tension between desiring closeness and fearing abandonment. As such, they experience emotional highs and lows with their relational partners. As you can imagine, both of these styles could have difficulty creating just relationships based on equity, respect, fair process, genuine dialogue, and other-centeredness. In contrast, those with *secure* attachment styles are comfortable with interdependence and closeness, and are able to trust others—all elements conducive to creating healthy, fair relationships.

NEGLECTED

by Shanae G.

(You **see**, I don't know if these men or women start to realize how much a man can affect a child's life to a point they start to feel neglected.)

My dad is starting to make me angry
People wonder why do I act so mean to guys
Maybe it's because I feel as if my father neglects me and doesn't take
    care of me or calls me
Makes me wonder why he do the things he do then That's when I start
    to think
This is how I treat my dudes
Un for real if he is sincere
Trying to give me love but I am not feeling it anymore
So why em I even writing this poem
Why em I even waiting for a phone call or for the day he's in sight
Maybe because I am mad I've finally come to realize that what he makes
    me feel is what I seem to look for in a guy
So it just seems right that I have a man
who doesn't visit me, conversating with me, locked in a cell room,
    no holiday spent with me, missing my birthday, giving me no
    hugs nor kiss
just the words how are you and checking on you
That's it!
My frustration is starting to feel like a bad trip with no love from the
    man who played a part in creating me but not raising me
Yall just don't understand!!!

I Am Angry With Men!

I am just not convinced that a good man exists because of this neglect-
    ing shit. So this is why I feel as no man deserves me because I don't
    want to be mistreated or mislead due to the ways I feel
That is why I want to tell my man that my love is unconditional and its
    true
I mean what I say and do what I mean; a man's word is everything to me
Hoping that my future man would come along and tell me
He does not doubt me but understand me
If I was ever to fall short then he'll hug me kiss me until I fully under-
    stood the meaning of real man love

> I just want some reassuring that he is what I want and not some illusion
> of what I am used to because this is the type of man that would be
> around my child
> *Most mothers don't think about who they date until it's too late, am
> not trying to be statistic am trying to escape.
>
> So I must worry because of my daughter I must make the right choice so my
> daughter doesn't fall into my footsteps cuz the man that helped me create
> her is doing exactly what my dad did to me neglecting her. It's just a repeat
> of history but maybe my second chances at love won't be a mistake it will
> be a man who changed my mind frame and reassured me that he wouldn't
> treat me the same.

Attribution Theory

Attributions influence our relational frames because in our attempt to understand "what caused something else" (Manusov & Spitzberg, 2008) we attribute causes of behaviors to our partners and their somewhat stable dispositions (personalities) or to variable external circumstances. It is basically the difference between attributing someone's being late to a party because they're the kind of person who is "always" late (personality attribution) or because there was an accident on the freeway (external circumstance attribution). An important example of the significance of this process comes from attribution researchers that study marriage. They have found that dissatisfied spouses tend to make *distress-maintaining* attributions, whereas happy couples make *relationship-enhancing* attributions. Essentially, dissatisfied partners develop a relationship frame that attributes the cause of the partners' actions to personality traits that are viewed as consistent and unchanging, whereas satisfied partners have a relationship frame that focuses on positive elements and de-emphasizes the negative (Manusov & Spitzberg, 2008). Of course, the potential effect of the first perspective is a relational frame of hopelessness ("He will never change"), whereas the potential effect of the second perspective is a relational frame of optimism ("I think that was just a bad time to try to talk about it").

An important lesson I learned during the practicum portion of my masters in counseling program was that people need *hope* to change. Relationship mythologies (as discussed in Chapter Two: "Just Relationships") can facilitate hopeful, relationship-enhancing messages or corrosive, distress-maintaining messages. A partner's relationship mythology embodies what he or she believes is "true" about the relationship—"He doesn't care or respect me. I am doomed to be unhappy if I stay in this relationship," as compared to, "I know he values our relationship and tries to show me respect." In essence, your relationship mythology reflects and shapes your relationship frame. If your relationship frame is distress-maintaining, you may typically display protecting behaviors because you don't feel safe with your partner. For example, threatening to

John and Susan have been struggling in their marriage for the past two years. John has been especially overworked the last two weeks, and when he came home late last night he spoke sharply to Susan:

> John: I saw an alert come through on my phone that you made a large purchase without consulting me. We can't afford that. I'm cutting you off!
> Susan: Speak to me like that again and I'm out of here!

Trish and Allison have been together for four years. Trish has also been overworked the last two weeks and, similar to John, speaks sharply to her partner when she comes home late from work:

> Trish: I saw an alert come through on my phone that you made a large purchase without consulting me. We can't afford that. I'm cutting you off!
> Allison: Your remark was hurtful. I want to talk about this, but at a time when we are both calmer.

leave is a defense mechanism many of us have used since we were young. On the other hand, if your frame is relationship-enhancing, you may experience hope and trust, and engage your partner in the co-creation of a just relationship. Consider the interactions in *Box 6.1*, one distress-maintaining, the other relationship-enhancing.

John and Susan have created a relationship frame over the past two years that is distress-maintaining. In particular they are operating under a couple of negative relationship myths: "Susan can't handle money," "John doesn't respect Susan." In contrast, Trish and Allison co-created a relational frame that is relationship-enhancing. Their positive relationship myths include: "We can get through anything when we take time to calm down before we talk" and "We solve problems when we're honest and caring."

Creating a Flexible Relational Frame

Certain types of relational frames inhibit the co-creation of just relationships. And, like all worldviews, these relational frames are resistant to change for at least two reasons. First, our worldviews consist of foundational assumptions about our existence that are connected to the many situation-specific beliefs that we hold. Practically, this means that for every foundational assumption I change, I have myriad situation-beliefs that have to be altered. For instance, at a foundational level, if my relationship frame is focused on love as the best way to create change in a specific situation (see Chapter Four: "Love Relationships"), I may choose kindness as a means to encourage change with my neighbor, instead of calling the police, because kindness is consistent with my foundational belief of love. However, if I instead choose to call the police, I have to reinterpret my foundational belief in love, or in some way rationalize my decision (e.g., calling the police *is* loving or love only works in long-term relationships). A second reason that relational frames (relational worldviews) resist change is that they are often deeply embedded in culture. To change my foundational belief is to go against my "tribe" (this idea is further developed in Chapter Seven: "Dehumanizing the 'Other'") creating personal uncertainty and possible conflict with those I identify with and love. In essence, changing one's relational frame, at the very least, requires a lot of effort, and at the most, generates anger, anxiety, and fear (Kaiser, Vick, & Major, 2004).

> *Living It Out: In Chapter Five: "Interpersonal Advocacy: Creating Spaces," I asked you and your partner, individually, to take time to think about your own worldviews— that is, how have you come to think about and experience the world as you have. Now, I want you to reflect on how you developed your worldview (e.g., family, past relationship experiences) and assess whether there are parts of this "relationship frame" that inhibit working with your relationship partner?*
>
> *Living It Out: Be proactive. Think through your relationship frame and be on the lookout for reasons it might be resistant to change.*

Relational Framing

As we have discussed, Relational Framing Theory highlights that people evaluate their interpersonal communication interactions either through a framework of control and submission or connection and distance. Of course, when we are correct in the way we see things (e.g., Miranda really is controlling), this is an efficient means of understanding relationships. However, when we pick up on early interaction cues and assign the wrong frame, or interpretation, to the interaction, it can create misunderstanding and a situation where we are resistant to change . . . because we think we are right. This is particularly problematic because your relational frame affects how you see things in the relationship—"You are not just trying to include me, you are trying to manipulate me . . . *like always!*" Being open to multiple relationship frames allows for greater openness and broader interpretation of relationship events and behavior.

> *Living It Out: Do you have a tendency to see things from one relationship frame (control-submission, connection-distance)? If so, think about how your tendency to see things through one relational frame might contribute to misunderstanding.*
>
> *Living It Out: When stuck in one relational frame, try out another even if it seems like it won't fit. For example, when you are using your dominance frame with your friend, try viewing the situation from a connection or protection standpoint and see if that makes a difference.*

Attachment Theory

Attachment theory proposes that we come to our adult relationships with a relationship mindset that is in part determined by our attachment, as infants, to our primary caregiver. Those with avoidant and anxious-ambivalent relational frames often struggle in their relationships, whereas securely attached individuals tend to have cooperative, trusting encounters. Relational hurt tends to bring up essential questions regarding our relationship mindsets (Feeney, 2009): Am I loveable? Will you be available when I need you? Will you be responsive? Can I trust you? As I previously emphasized, these questions influence our relational frames and affect our ability to construct *just relationships*.

> *Living It Out: Be careful not to place yourself too firmly in one of the nonsecure attachment categories. None of us had perfect upbringings. And, for the record, no matter what you've done (or not done)—You are loveable! If you struggle with this idea, write down, "I am loveable" or "I am worth it," and put it in your purse or wallet. When you're feeling down, pull it out and read it out loud. Remember, good relationships are built on healthy partners.*
>
> *Living It Out: Think about the four questions that come up when people are hurt (Am I loveable? Will you be available when I need you? Will you be responsive? Can I trust you?). Are these questions you've dealt with? Do you think your answers to these questions represent an accurate view of you? Of your partner?*

Attribution Theory

Attribution theorists focus on how we attribute cause to behaviors or events—was it your (or my) fault or some external circumstance? Is it likely to happen again? One important finding that attribution researchers have discussed is that dissatisfied partners tend to create distress-maintaining cycles of behavior and thinking, whereas satisfied partners' behavior and thinking is relationship-enhancing. These relational frames influence our ability to maintain healthy, just relationships.

> *Living It Out: Identify one or two of your relationship mythologies. That is, what are the key things (positive or negative) that you hold on to as "true" about your relationship? ("We are great companions," "We talk a lot," "We can never discuss anything without fighting," "We are great sexual partners," "We are too different to ever be truly happy.") Do you think these mythologies are distress-maintaining or relationship enhancing? (Remember, relationship mythologies may be factual, or not, but they always reveal something believed to be true about your relationship.)*
>
> *Living It Out: Discuss your relationship mythologies with your partner. How can you change your mythologies so that they might enhance your relationship, instead of maintain a cycle of distress?*

Framing Recollections

Adlerian psychologists use a technique called *early recollections* to determine how clients view themselves and others (Pomeroy & Clark, 2015). Though they may not directly use the term "worldview" these recollections are intended to provide insight into the client's worldview. After a client reveals a couple of her early recollections, an

Adlerian therapist may offer a phrase that summarizes some particular perspective. The phrase could be something like, "Life is a place where . . ." "Women are . . ." "Relationships can be . . ." When the client hears something that rings true, she uses the phrase to process choices she makes. We can all do something similar to help us understand our relationship frame. I call this process *framing recollections*.

> *Living It Out: As a way of better understanding you and your partner's relationship frame, answer the following questions and then share them with your partner over dinner! This isn't time for judging or determining who has the "right" responses, rather use genuine dialogue to understand and affirm one another more fully, and to appreciate how your similarities and differences might affect your relationship.*
>
> *Relationships are . . .*
> *Women are . . .*
> *Men are . . .*
> *Love is . . .*
> *Closeness is . . .*
> *Control is . . .*
> *Trust is . . .*
> *Parents are . . .*
> *Friends are . . .*
> *Add your own . . .*

Case 6.1

Katie is struggling after breaking up with Matt—for good, this time. Their nine-month relationship has been characterized by a cycle of break-up and make-up, typically generated by Katie's jealousy over Matt talking to other women. Each time she breaks up with Matt she talks with her friends, grieving the loss, missing him terribly, and fearing she has made a terrible mistake. She thinks he is a "player," but she loves him and thinks she can change him. Her friends, on the other hand, see Matt as controlling and often try to talk Katie into staying out of the relationship. However, Katie doesn't seem to be able to *not* contact Matt for long. Inevitably, within a week she ends up texting Matt, apologizing for her jealousy and asking him to take her back. It typically takes a couple days, but Matt eventually agrees and they end up dating again. Predictably, a month later the whole process repeats itself.

Processing . . .

1. How do you think Katie and Matt are each framing their relationship interactions (control-submission, connection-distance)?

2. Reflecting on attachment theory, do you think Katie is securely attached? How would Katie answer key attachment theory questions: Am I loveworthy? Is Matt available to me? Is he responsive? Is he trustworthy?

3. Describe the interaction patterns that characterize Katie and Matt's communication. Are they relationship-enhancing or distress-maintaining?

4. Fill in two of the phrases, described in *Framing Recollections,* that you think are important to Katie and Matt.

Case 6.2

On his drive home from the Pinal County Jail, Ramon was troubled. He had been visiting Martin, a 17-year-old young man, who had committed his first felony—stealing a car. Martin grew up in a household that included his mom, older brother, and younger sister. Martin's mom worked hard, but over the years she brought a number of men into their household, creating a great deal of instability and uncertainty for Martin. Over time, he began to close off to the next potential "father-figure" because each man ended up leaving after a few months, and Martin would end up hurt, once again. He also began to resent his mother—"Why can't we kids be enough for her?" Martin's older brother had dropped out of school in seventh grade, joined a gang, and at age 21 had already spent two years in prison. Martin made it through eighth grade, but the allure of belonging to a gang where he had a purpose, and there were "older men" (most in their early 20s) who affirmed him, was stronger than the hopelessness of home life. Martin began to believe that there were few people he could trust and much of life was doing your best to stay in control.

Ramon knew Martin's story well. In fact, he had grown up in the hood, himself, and watched others go down this path. Ramon had heavily invested in Martin's life since he first met him as a fifth-grader at South Mountain Christian Church, where Ramon served as the children and youth pastor. Ramon was grieving over what Martin had done and the consequences he would have to pay—to Ramon, it was such a waste for such a "good kid." But, he was also frustrated that Ramon could make such a mistake after all the time they had spent together—all the retreats and teaching about how to live a "good" life. He was certain that Martin "knew better" than to have stolen a car. However, what really bothered Ramon was the way the conversation ended—Martin looked him in the eye and said, "I was going to end up here, anyway. This is where my brother has been, and probably my "real" father, too. At least, now, I have some street cred," and then turned and walked away.

Processing . . .

1. Reflecting on attachment theory, do you think Martin is securely attached? How would Martin answer key attachment theory questions: Am I loveworthy? Is anyone available to me? Is anyone responsive? Is there anyone I can trust?

2. What relationship frames do you think are most important to Martin (e.g., control-submission, connection-distance)?
3. Discuss how Martin is viewing life as either relationship-enhancing (you could also think of this as "life-enhancing") or distress-maintaining. How might he change the parts of his thinking that maintain a cycle of distress?
4. How might Martin answer some of the following relational frame questions? Relationships are . . . Men are . . . Control is . . . Trust is . . .

References

Bulman-Janoff, R. (1989). Assumptive worlds and the stress of traumatic events: Application of the schema construct. *Social Cognition, 7*(2), 113–136.

Feeney, J. A. (2005). Hurt feelings in couple relationships: Exploring the role of attachment and perceptions of personal injury. *Personal Relationships, 12,* 255–271.

Feeney, J. A. (2009). When love hurts: Understanding hurtful events in couple relationships. In A. Vangelisti (Ed.), *Feeling hurt in close relationships* (pp. 313–335). New York: Cambridge University Press.

Haste, H., & Abrahams, S. (2008). Morality, culture and the dialogic self: Taking cultural pluralism seriously. *Journal of Moral Education, 37*(3), 377–394. http://www.tandfonline.com/. . ./03057240802227502

Hazan, C., & Shaver, P. (1987). Romantic love conceptualized as an attachment process. *Journal of Personality and Social Psychology, 52*(3), 511–524.

Kaiser, C. R., Vick, S. B., & Major, B. (2004). A prospective investigation of the just-world beliefs and the desire for revenge after September 11, 2001. *Psychological Science, 15*(7), 503–506.

Kluckhohn, F. R. (1950). Dominant and substitute profiles of cultural orientations: Their significance for the analysis of social stratification. *Social Forces, 28,* 376–393.

Manusov, V., & Spitzberg, B. H. (2008). Attributes of attribution theory: Finding good cause in the search for theory. In D. O. Braithwaite & L. A. Baxter (Eds.), *Engaging theories in interpersonal communication* (pp. 37–49). Thousand Oaks, CA: Sage.

Mead, S. (2014). http://www.intentionalpeersupport.org/wp-content/uploads/2014/12/IPS-An-Alternative-Approach-2014-First-Chapter.pdf

Pomeroy, H., & Clark, A. J. (2015). Self-efficacy and early recollections in the context of Adlerian and wellness theory. *Journal of Individual Psychology, 71,* 24–35.

Rivera-Koltko, M. E. (2004). The psychology of worldviews. *Review of General Psychology, 8*(1), 3–58. doi: 0.1037/1089–2680.8.1.3

Solomon, D. H., & McLaren, R. M. (2008). Relational framing theory: Drawing inferences about relationships from interpersonal interactions. In L. A. Baxter & D. O. Braithwaite (Eds.), *Engaging theories in interpersonal communication: Multiple perspectives* (pp. 103–115). Thousand Oaks, CA: Sage.

Trees, A. R. (2006). Attachment theory: The reciprocal relationship between family communication and attachment patterns. In D. O. Braithwaite & L. A. Baxter (Eds.), *Engaging theories in family communication: Multiple perspectives* (pp. 163–161). Thousand Oaks: Sage.

7

DEHUMANIZING THE "OTHER"

"This is my tribe"—a common phrase in some circles. It means, we are family, this is my team, my ingroup. We are social beings. We all have a need to be part of a tribe. Tribal in this sense has many positive connotations—connection, cohesion, closeness, protection. In fact, this sort of ingroup thinking is related to positive outcomes such as self-esteem and positive self-concept (Merola & McGlone, 2011). Belonging to a group that is valued by myself and others reinforces my own self-worth. Yet, tribes can also be characterized by ingroup thinking that dehumanizes other persons and groups. For example, Merola and McGlone (2011) have researched Cherokee tribes in North America that term themselves *Ani Yun'wiya* (the "principle people") and the Yup'ik in Alaska who view themselves as the "real people," and concluded that these names imply a lessening of the "humanness" of others—that is, others are less principle or central, or less real.

Dehumanization is a consequence of maintaining a worldview, a *relationship frame* (Chapter Six: "Worldview: Your Relationship Frame"), that limits our ability to work toward establishing just relationships. In essence, when a significant aspect of our own well-being is based on our group being *better than* (more human than . . .) your group, treating you with respect and a sense of equality becomes an elusive goal.

Dehumanization

Dehumanization has been conceptualized in a variety of forms. Two prominent ways in which individuals view one another as nonhuman are by using a mechanistic or animalistic (Haslam, 2006) relationship frame. When we use a mechanistic frame to view others we strip them of the human elements of warmth, nurturing, and affection. Machines are objects to be used for a purpose, without a sense of deeper meaning. When we maintain a friendship only for what we get from it (e.g., you always take me to the airport, but that's our only contact with each other), we are treating one another in a mechanistic way. In addition, machines are impervious to pain; when they have served their purpose, they can be cast aside. An adolescent who is struggling with her parents may see them from this mechanistic relational frame—unaware that they have feelings, and mostly using them for food and shelter.

Viewing others from an animalistic perspective also strips them of human characteristics, but animalistic dehumanization fails to see others in terms of their moral ethic and culture and, instead, sees them as impulsive, unpredictable, and dangerous. As I am writing this chapter, the United States is debating whether to take in Syrian refugees. It is possible in our efforts to keep America "safe," to dehumanize these refugee families by seeing them as dangerous and unpredictable, and by failing to understand their culture and morality (for instance, many of the refugees are families in which the parents are hoping to find a safe place to raise their children). Thus, animalistic dehumanization leads us to either bring "animals" (those who are different from us) under control or live in such a way that we are protected from them—typically this means restricting their access to us or using violence.

Humans as Emotional Beings

Animals, in the sense we have been discussing them, are not human, but they do have certain qualities akin to human experience. In particular, higher-order mammals are able to express a range of emotion. When we treat others as though they only have access to a limited range of emotion, we limit their humanity—this process is called infrahumanization. In this regard, social scientists have distinguished between primary and secondary emotions (Leyens et al., 2000). Primary emotions are the center of our affective experience. Primary emotions, such as fear, happiness, and sadness, are "direct, spontaneous responses to stimuli in the immediate environment" (Merola & McGlone, 2011, p. 326). These become the foundation of secondary-emotion responses, such as indignation, shame, and pride. Secondary emotions are "indirect, reflective responses to objects and people that need not be physically present" (p. 326). Thus, secondary emotions are more reflexive and complex than their primary counterparts and, as such, linked most strongly to the unique human experience.

Denying that certain people or groups experience the full range of primary and secondary emotions dehumanizes them. For example, in Chapter One: "Just Thoughts" I share a quote from Debbie who talks about the shame of her undocumented husband. Her recognition of this secondary emotion demonstrates that she sees her husband as fully human. Others of us, however, may only have associated primary emotions with undocumented individuals (e.g., fear of being caught). Thus, one way to justify inhuman behavior toward others is to view them with a relational frame that filters out their experience of secondary emotions. Work by Merola and McGlone (2011) focuses on how infrahumanization is represented in communication behavior. Their examination of prolife and prochoice blogs reveals "a reliable tendency among both groups to attribute primary but not secondary emotions to their adversaries" (p. 323). When writing about ingroup members, bloggers were more likely to recognize complex emotions such as pride and disdain, as compared to when they wrote about outgroup members who tended to be viewed more simply as happy or angry. Although this distinction may initially seem to be a minor one, the process of infrahumanization may significantly influence our perceptions of others as human and, as such, may lead to increased discrimination of those in outgroups, as well as less willingness to forgive (Leyens, Demoulin, Vaes, Gaunt, & Paladino, 2007).

Ethnocentrism

Ethnocentrism is a worldview, or relationship frame (Chapter Six: "Worldview: Your Relationship Frame"), that only allows one to "see" through one's own cultural perspective. Resultant ingroup effects can lead to seeing others as less than fully human. This process takes place at both macro (societal) and micro (relationship) levels. For example, at a macro level my own personal worldview is influenced by the fact that I am American. As such, I tend to view events as they relate to individualism and freedom and may view those who do not hold these same values as less than fully human. I also view marriage as something that occurs between two individuals who are free and autonomous to make their own choices in the relationship. As such, I tend to be judgmental of heterosexual relationships wherein women are not treated as equals. Similarly, at a micro level, my relationship frame is shaped by my experience of humor and play in my own marriage. I don't fully understand, or may even be judgmental of, marriages that do not appear to value fun.

Ethnocentrism can be useful to help groups shape their own identities and create a sense of internal cohesion—we like and value who we are as a group. Family is an example where ethnocentrism (viewing our family as a microculture) can function to bring us together. However, ethnocentric thinking often comes at a significant price. The ethnocentric relational frame often devalues others as a way of bolstering one's own group identity. In essence, I see what we do as a family as "better" than what you do as a family. Leyens et al. (2007) state that "To be ethnocentric means that one's group is by definition superior on a variety of dimensions and that outgroups lack a number of important characteristics to be comparable to the ingroup" (p. 141). This process often leads to subtle, or not so subtle, judgments of other groups and people, because they have fewer of the qualities that one's ingroup considers to be most human.

Change and Imagination

Atrocities in South Africa before 1994 were embedded in a skewed worldview where certain groups of people viewed other groups as less than fully human. Oelofsen (2009) writes about such atrocities and suggests that dehumanization is rooted in the perception that certain persons, or groups of people, are incapable of change. Consistent with our previous discussion, we may discard machines (mechanistic perspective) or control or put down animals (animalistic perspective) when we think they can't be changed, or adapt, to fit how we think they should function. Once when we were having trouble with our cat a friend of mine offered, "When the cat is no longer making you happy, put it down." In essence, nonpersons don't change and should be discarded when they don't meet *my* expectations or desires, whereas "persons" respond in creative ways to their environments and, as such, I may engage them in dialogue and collaborative planning and behavior. When we respond to others as if they are capable of growth, change, and adaptation we respond humanely.

As we saw in Chapter Six: "Worldview: Your Relationship Frame," by making negative, stable, personality-based attributions about our partners, we maintain a relationship frame that is distress-maintaining (e.g., "She'll never change!"; Manusov & Spitzberg, 2008). In this sense, distress-maintaining perceptions dehumanize the other person by visualizing them as a mass of fixed characteristics with no hope for adaptation and change. On the other hand, relationship-enhancing perceptions reflect the inherent humanness of others because they recognize the situational constraints that others are working with and that as humans they are capable of adapting to various situational contingencies. In essence, they see their human brothers and sisters as able to learn and respond in innovative ways, as opposed to being locked into an unchanging personality.

Consistent with this attribution-based thinking, imagination has been linked to positive relationship outcomes and humanizing our relational partners. Researchers are finding that relational happiness is associated with pleasant imagined interactions. For example, Honeycutt and Wiemann (1999) found that engaged partners who cultivate positive imagined interactions with their fiancé are happy with their relationships. These findings, coupled with research on distress-maintaining and relationship-enhancing perceptions, strongly suggest that the relationship frame through which we choose to view others has a significant influence on our ability to work toward creating and maintaining just relationships. As Oelofsen (2009) suggests, our ability to imagine (to change our relationship frame) is at the very heart of rehumanization. She suggests that imagination is central to empathy, the ability to see others' problems and pains and, as such, "linked to dehumanization as indifference, as it is a lack of imagination which allows indifference in the face of atrocities" (p. 183).

Building Healthy Tribes . . . Rehumanizing Ourselves and Others

We humanize others when we treat them as complex individuals who experience a rich, broad range of emotions and are capable of adaptation and change. To treat others in this manner signals our equal worth and our mutual value of growth and process. By definition, to humanize others, and ourselves, is inherently moral (see Chapter Three: "Good Relationships").

Tribalism and ethnocentrism often restrict our humanizing responses. With time, these ingroup processes may compromise our ability to see others' complexity and potential for change and growth. Yet, *imagination*, expanding our relational frame, opens the possibility to creatively understand our relational partners (Oelofsen, 2009). When embraced, this new understanding leads to empathy and love, and compassionate responses that are truly centered on the well-being of the other.

Although it may seem counterintuitive, the beginning point of rehumanization is self-awareness—how did I get where I am at (psychologically, relationally, socio-economically), and how do others see me? Second, I become aware of my own tendency toward infrahumanization and ethnocentrism. Third, imagination facilitates my understanding of how others' experience of life is different from my own, that is, different from my tribe's, but also similar in ways (e.g., we both want to raise healthy children). Finally, we co-create patterns that keep both of us adaptable and imaginative.

Self-Awareness

Oelofsen's (2009) conceptualization of rehumanization includes two aspects that increase our self-awareness. First, we see ourselves in historical context. I try to understand myself within my own cultural context or, for our purposes here, within my various relationship contexts. Oelofsen suggests that this early part of rehumanizing the other could require us to "re-forge" our own identities (p. 186). Second, we must learn to see ourselves as others see us. If this conflicts with our own self-perception, we must investigate why others see us this way. Why might someone see us as oppressive, controlling, insensitive, or hurtful?

> *Living It Out: As we have done earlier in this book, revisit how you've become who you are. What do you like, or dislike, about your "self" within your particular cultural or relational setting? To do this, select one cultural group you are part of (e.g., your family, work, religion, gender, ethnicity, sexual orientation . . .). Write about a time when you felt like you fit in this group and a time when you felt like you didn't fit. What did you like or dislike about fitting/not-fitting?*
>
> *Living It Out: Reflect on why some people might view you negatively. If you're struggling with this, think of words people have used, at times, to describe you in negative terms (controlling, passive, irritating, a victim . . .). Now, think about what it is in their background that influences them to see your behavior negatively. (Be careful when doing this. The goal here is not to damage your self-esteem, but to give you insight as to other people's legitimate ways of viewing things.)*
>
> *Living It Out: Ok, now let's re-forge parts of our own identities. Based on the first two "Living It Out" segments, is it possible to begin viewing aspects of yourself in a new way? (After deep talks with a friend of mine, he had to re-forge his identity as actually being sensitive to other people. Another friend, after rethinking her past, re-forged her identity as being competent!)*

Awareness of our Own Infrahumanizing Tendencies

Most of us are barely aware of our own relational frames. As such, once we've become more aware of our own cultural and relational context, our task is to bring into focus our tendencies to dehumanize, or infrahumanize, others. As we have discussed, viewing others as incapable of change is a key element of seeing others as less than fully human (Oelofsen, 2009). Being able to change is essential to the notion that we are autonomous and free, capable of making our own choices, adapting and growing. When we respond to others as though growth and change are no longer legitimate options, we are treating them as less than human. This type of thinking also legitimizes treating others in a morally different way than we treat those we deem as our equals. This may involve failing to recognize their experience of secondary emotions. As such, we treat infrahumanized others as though they are nonreflective of their own (less-than) human journey and only experience emotions at a basic, animalistic level.

I became poignantly aware of de- and infrahumanization when one of my teaching assistants shared with our class examples of statements said to her as a lesbian woman— "What a waste," "Who's the boy and who's the girl?" "It's just a phase," "Butch." These comments fail to take into account her reflexive and complex experience of emotions as she explores and embraces her own sexuality. They fail to see her as a growing, changing human being. Even the phrase, "It's just a phase," fails to recognize her humanity as a change agent, but rather keeps her locked into one way of experiencing her life.

> *Living It Out: Think of labels you use to describe others: lazy, selfish, lame, nerd . . . or, perhaps, thoughtful, flexible, responsive. How do these labels indicate that you view other persons as either static and unchanging or growing and adaptable?*
>
> *Living It Out: Think of a relationship wherein you view the other person as "static," nonchanging (you think they will never "get it," or they will always be "hot-headed"). Write down one to three ways in which this "static" view of your partner inhibits your ability to treat them with respect. Follow up by viewing this person as "dynamic" and "changing". How might this alter the way you relate to him or her? (For example, how would changing, "She'll never change," to "She is growing in her own way," influence how you interact with your mom?)*

Imaginative Understanding

Ethnocentrism occurs when we restrict our view of others through our own cultural frame. It can provide certain ingroup benefits (cohesion and joint identity) but, without seeing others from a variety of perspectives, often results in thinking of ourselves as better (more fully and uniquely human) than others. In contrast, we can attempt to imaginatively understand our relational partners from within their own personal journey. When we imagine the other person from his or her own perspective, we see the other person "in context" (Oelofsen, 2009). This is the final step in restoring the human element—"My gosh, if I had grown up like him . . ."

"I didn't realize that she had suffered so much pain regarding . . ." "What if no one had ever loved or affirmed me or . . . ?"

Viewing others from their own perspective creates a sense of empathy. This is very different from the sympathy we feel when we observe others' suffering from our own independent space. With empathy we imaginatively experience how someone else thinks and feels. Responding compassionately to this new sense of the other creates an other-centered response that positively affects the relationship (Chapter Four: "Love Relationships"). In essence, imagination-based empathy and other-centeredness is a moral response that engages others and facilitates our mutual humanity.

> *Living It Out: This week, when you are with others who are different from you in some significant way, take note of how your own ethnocentric beliefs have limited your ability to see their perspective.*
>
> *Living It Out: In a conversation where the other person's perspective "makes no sense" to you, seek to understand the other person's perspective. Don't ask, "Why?" but rather ask for elaboration and clarification. Be interested, curious, not defensive (think back to the mindful exercises we engaged in previous chapters).*
>
> *Living It Out: What would it be like today to feel empathy for someone else? Is there a way that your empathy can turn itself into compassionate action?*
>
> *Living It Out: Think about your partner or a person you're in conflict with. Take time to write about how you think they see their own situation. Then, whether you agree or disagree with their perspective, decide that their perspective is valid.*

Encouraging Imagination and Change

At one point, ten years or so into my marriage, I wrote a poem for my wife, entitled, *Afraid to Let You Grow*. Ann and I were going through a difficult time and I suddenly realized that I was afraid to let her grow. Somehow her growth, her change, seemed threatening to me. I only knew how to do our relationship in one way. I had a tribalistic relationship frame—anything other than what I knew was "bad." I was insecure managing uncertainty and change. Without fully understanding what I was doing, writing the poem for my wife was my attempt at initiating a genuine dialogue with her—creating a space where we might be vulnerably present with each other. Oelofsen (2009) tells us that imagination is critical to dialogue. As we've seen previously, dialogue is a central means of contributing to one another's discovery of our own humanity (Baxter, 2004). Honest dialogue *creates a space where if something good can happen, it will* (Chapter Five: "Interpersonal Advocacy"). In overcoming our tendencies toward dehumanization, we create a safe space for complex expression of ourselves and mutual change. We humanize others as we recognize and encourage their change, their growth. We humanize ourselves as we embrace our own growth and change.

> *Living It Out: Think about a relationship that you are in. Are you exhibiting actions and responses that are possibly keeping your partner "stuck"?*

Living It Out: Is there some way your partner has been wanting to grow and change? Could you ask your partner, while respecting their autonomy, if there is a way you can help facilitate this change?

Living It Out: How about really getting out of the box and writing a poem for your partner? The goal isn't to be a great poet. The goal is to find common language to share something that is otherwise hard to express. If poetry isn't your thing, share song lyrics, a drawing or painting, or even a picture you've taken with your phone that represents what you are thinking and feeling.

Case 7.1

Gabe and Christi divorced a year ago. Christi was very hurt by the divorce, which was initiated by Gabe. Because she and Gabe had both worked hard during their 15-year marriage, they had not taken time to develop much social support from friends and family relations. They mostly worked and spent time with their 13-year-old daughter, Sabrina. After the divorce, Christi gained custody of Sabrina. As Christi grappled with her own emotional pain, she shared with Sabrina about Gabe's shortcomings and failings. She described him as someone who was insensitive to her needs. He was mostly happy, but he didn't really understand her and seemed unable to feel much emotion. She tried talking to him, but eventually thought, "He'll never change." From Christi's perspective, Gabe was just like his dad—Gabe's dad was a "good man" without much sensitivity. Christi shared all of this with Sabrina, in part because she had no one else to share with, and in part to draw closer to Sabrina.

Sabrina, who loved both her father and mother, didn't know what to do with this information. She knew her dad (Gabe) wasn't perfect, but she loved him and believed that he loved her, too, even though he was awkward at showing it. It seemed to her that he tried to be a good dad and, she assumed, a good husband.

Processing

1. How did Christi dehumanize Gabe as she talked with Sabrina?
2. How did Sabrina see Gabe as more human than did Christi?
3. How did Gabe dehumanize Christi during their marriage (at least from Christi's perspective)?
4. How might Christi's "honesty" with Sabrina potentially damage their relationship?
5. How might imaginative understanding help Sabrina better understand her dad and her mom?

Case 7.2

Victor was a part of a local gang in Albuquerque; Luis was a member of a rival gang. Luis had heard stories about Victor. In a way, he respected him. But, he would never put words to that respect. His Spanish-only-speaking gang would not tolerate any sense of "softening" toward a rival gang member—other gangs were "animals" that were threats to Luis's gang. Likewise, Victor knew of Luis, but only considered him as a threat to maintaining his own territory.

Years later, after becoming a member of a local community organization, Victor and a prison mentor visited inmates at the local jail. He audibly caught his breath when he saw Luis. He knew that in another setting Luis would have killed him, but Victor chose to walk up to Luis and shake his hand. Following this encounter, Luis had a short conversation with the mentor, and then Victor and the mentor left the jail. Months later, shortly after Luis's release, Luis and Victor met face-to-face at a weekly meeting for the community organization to which they both belonged. They each stopped in their tracks, looking straight into the other's eyes. Luis imagined what it must have been like for Victor to come up to him in the jail, and then made the first move. Luis walked slowly toward Victor, gave him a bro-hug, and thanked him for connecting in the jail. Victor told him to "forget about it," but Luis never did. Today they work side by side with the same community organization. (Adapted from *The Relentless Pursuit: Stories of God's Hope, Love and Grace in the Neighborhood* by Sherman, 2007.)

1. How did Luis dehumanize (infrahumanize) Victor? How did Victor dehumanize (infrahumanize) Luis?
2. How were Luis and Victor "stuck" in terms of recognizing the other as "human"?
3. How do you think Victor or Luis might have gone through (or did go through) the process of rehumanization to change their own perspectives of the other?

References

Baxter, L. A. (2004). Dialogues of relating. In R. Anderson, L. A. Baxter, & K. N. Cissna (Eds.), *Dialogue: Theorizing difference in communication studies* (pp. 107–124). Thousand Oaks, CA: Sage.

Haslam, N. (2006). Dehumanization: An integrated review. *Personality and Social Psychology Review, 10*(3), 252–264.

Honeycutt, J. M., & Wiemann, J. M. (1999). Analysis of functions of talk and reports of imagined interactions (IIs) during engagement and marriage. *Human Communication Research, 25*, 399–419.

Leyens, J. P., Demoulin, S., Vaes, J., Gaunt, R., & Paladino, M. P. (2007). Infra-humanization: The wall of group differences. *Social Issues and Policy Review, 1*(1), 139–172.

Leyens, J. P., Paladino, M. P., Rodriguez, R. T., Vaes, J., Demoulin, S., Rodriguez, A. P., & Gaunt, R. (2000). The emotional side of prejudice: The role of secondary emotions. *Personality and Social Psychology Review, 4*, 186–197.

Manusov, V., & Spitzberg, B. H. (2008). Attributes of attribution theory: Finding good cause in the search for theory. In D. O. Braithwaite & L. A. Baxter (Eds.), *Engaging theories in interpersonal communication* (pp. 37–49). Thousand Oaks, CA: Sage Publications.

Merola, N. A., & McGlone, M. S. (2011). Adversarial infrahumanization in the abortion debate. *Western Journal of Communication, 75*(3), 323–340. doi: 10.1080/10570314.2011.571651

Oelofsen, R. (2009). De- and rehumanization in the wake of atrocities. *South African Journal of Philosophy, 28*(2), 178–188.

Sherman, A. L. (2007). *The relentless pursuit: Stories of God's hope, love, and grace in the neighborhood.* Colorado Springs, CO: Dawson Media.

8

SAVING FACE

Erving Goffman (1959) creatively conceived the human endeavor as one in which individuals play "parts," as though on a stage. Imagine watching early Greek theater where actors and actresses speak their lines behind masks or, literally, faces. Each "face" represents a role or emotion that the individual actor plays and experiences within the larger context of the play itself—tragedy or comedy. In the same way, each of us adopts particular personas from which we enact specific behaviors and emotions in our various relationships. Over time we develop a substantial investment in maintaining the "face" that represents each of the roles we play. And, inevitably, there are times when our face concerns become the primary focus of conversations and limit our abilities to interact with others in ways that are fair, just, and human. As such, it is critical that we learn to protect and enhance face, ours and our partners', in ways that allow us to work together as equals.

I would describe a friend of mine, Manny, as a likeable poser. I care about him, greatly, and enjoy his company. But, he is always busy maintaining his face. I feel like I never get beyond his mask, beyond his posing as whatever character he chooses to play. Take, for example, the other day when Manny and I met at a sports bar to watch some of the NCAA's March Madness. I knew some tough things were going on in his life, but when I asked how he was doing I felt like he put on his "competence" mask, "There are hard things, but I have them under control," "I'm learning some things from this, so it's all good," "These things wouldn't be happening except for Judy's inability to manage money." As the topics shifted and we watched the basketball games, Manny continued to feed me a steady stream of "I'm knowledgeable," "I'm competent," "I'm good" responses. In spite of evidence to the contrary, he spoke as if he had his life under control, and . . . was even smarter than the coaches, the referees, and the players we were watching in the final four—amazing!

This example demonstrates that when we are primarily invested in saving face, we lose access to the humanness that is the core of who we are as persons. The result of my time with Manny was constant posturing about what each of us knew about basketball, instead of a deeper conversation about what Manny was really dealing with. In this chapter, I present the idea of *face* and its importance in limiting or facilitating genuine dialogue with our relational partners.

Face, Facework, and Goals of Interaction

All of us have social faces that we are emotionally connected to and protect. Face essentially is "The conception of self that each person displays in particular interactions with others" (Cupach & Metts, 1994). As we interact with others we enact our goal of *face confirmation* by presenting a particular idea of our "self" that we hope others will affirm. As such, our face is in constant flux. As we communicate we make continuous adjustments relative to our partner and contingencies in the interaction. Over time, our face is confirmed or disconfirmed, enhanced or threatened.

To better understand how face works, let's take a quick look at how face fits within the family of interaction goals (Canary, Cunningham, & Cody, 1988; Oetzel, Garcia, & Ting-Toomey, 2007). For our purposes I am going to describe interaction goals as: verbal topic, relationship, and identity or face goals. Often, the most evident of the goals is verbal topic. *Verbal topic goals* are instrumental in nature. They represent what might be termed the "primary end" of the verbal message. For instance, if I ask you, "Are you busy Friday night, because I'm flying to Reno and wondered if you could take me to the airport?", the most evident goal or topic of the statement is my desire for you to help me get to the airport. However, you may also be aware of a second, more relational, goal. *Relationship goals* may be expressed verbally; however, they most often are negotiated indirectly at the nonverbal level. In the preceding example, the fact that I feel like I can ask you to take me to the airport says something about how I see our relationship. However, if my request for you to take me to the airport was accompanied by "puppy dog eyes" or a tag-on statement ("take me to the airport . . . like you're never able to do"), you have additional cues that this message is not just about getting to my flight—it is also negotiating or testing whether I have the right or ability to *guilt* you into doing something for me. It may, in fact, also be a veiled attempt at negotiating the relational hurt I have felt when you haven't been able to help me.

Identity goals are connected to relational goals. Embedded in relationship goals are how I see myself and how I see you within the context of the relationship (Burgoon & Hale, 1984). It is important to recognize that identity goals represent who we think we are (personal, relational, and community identities; Domenici & Littlejohn, 2006) and *face goals* are oriented to how we present ourselves to others (Cupach & Metts, 1994). Identity and face are related in that face (self-presentational) goals arise when we need to protect, maintain, or develop our private sense of self (identity) or manage our public image for some other reason, such as meeting cultural (e.g., attending a family wedding) or organizational norms (e.g., conducting oneself during a job interview). Using the preceding example regarding taking me to the airport, my attempt at guilt-making may have called your private identity into question and generated an attempt to save public face on your part, "Hey wait a minute! It's not my fault you always wait until the last minute to ask me to help!"

As partners communicate with one another, topic, relationship, and identity goals advance and recede in each partner's awareness. As face goals come into awareness, individuals select communication strategies to create, preserve, or challenge a given face. Facework is the manner in which we communicate in order to create and maintain the three faces that are present during any given interaction: our own face (self-face), our partner's face (other-face), and our mutual face, which is concern for both partners' faces and concern for the relationship image (face) itself. To better understand the relationship between the three faces, consider Eriko, a mid-year transfer student and new roommate to Taylor. When Eriko first meets Taylor, she is concerned with creating and maintaining a particular public image (self-face). In her attempt to be seen as likeable, competent and, of course, cool, Eriko inadvertently says something that is heard negatively by Taylor (damaging other-face). Eriko senses that Taylor starts to shut down and become more cautious in her communication (self-face saving by Taylor) and, as such, tries to help preserve Taylor's face (other-face) by complimenting what she is wearing. Taylor appreciates Eriko's other-face preservation attempts, and the two of them begin maintaining their new found mutual face by talking about how they are the same size and are all about sharing clothes with one another.

Facework During Conflict

We are often unaware of our identity goals during interactions until we experience a potential threat to our face. Face threats occur "when a message has the potential to damage a person's preferred image" (Knobloch, Satterlee, & DiDomenico, 2010, p. 304). The potential damage from a face threat creates uncertainty and influences how we communicate with our relationship partners, often shifting the focus of an interaction from verbal content to relationship and identity goals. In other words, when our face is threatened, we quit focusing on finding a "fair" solution and, instead, work at protecting our face.

An interesting study by Oetzel et al. (2007) looked at this process. They examined facework in conflict situations across four different cultures (Chinese, Japanese, Germany, and US national cultures). Facework was categorized as *avoiding* (giving in, pretending, and using a third party), *dominating* (defending, expressing feelings, direct/passive aggression), and *integrating* (apologizing, private discussion, remaining calm, problem-solving, showing respect). Their findings showed few differences by culture (in other words, we all work to protect our face), however, they successfully demonstrated that facework takes different forms depending on the type of face that is of primary concern during the interaction. When participants were mostly concerned with their partner's face (other-face) they were likely to use avoiding or integrating strategies, such as remaining calm, apologizing, giving in and pretending there is no conflict, having private discussions, using third parties, and restricting the expression of negative emotions. When participants reported being concerned with their own face, they used more dominating strategies such as defending themselves and being more aggressive. When face concern was mutual (both partners' face or concern for the relationship) there was less expression of aggression and, instead, individuals expressed calm and respect, and attempted to problem solve, give in, and have private discussions. These findings suggest that mutual face awareness is very much related to creating processual justice (Chapter Two: "Just Relationships") in our personal relationships.

Facework: Prevention and Repair

Facework can be preventive or corrective (Cupach & Metts, 1994). When individuals fear possible face-threatening responses, they often protect by choosing one of three face-preserving strategies: avoidance, disclaimer, or politeness. Avoidance strategies include evading topics, changing topics during conversation, and simply pretending not to notice a face-threatening statement. Disclaimers are statements intended to minimize potential negative attributions of one's statements or behaviors, for example, "I may be wrong, but . . ." or "Hear me out before you get upset" Cupach & Metts, 1994, p. 7). Politeness strategies often involve being indirect to avoid seeming insensitive to one's partner, for example, "When you get time, could you please put your clothes away? I would so appreciate it" as opposed to, "I need YOU to pick up your clothes!"

Corrective facework is an attempt to repair damage done by a transgression in the relationship. You might choose to save your own face or the face of your relational partner when face has been compromised by another person's words or actions. You may also try to save your own face when you have said something face-threatening to others. Following I discuss eight strategies identified by Cupach and Metts (1994) that may be used to save face. *Avoidance*, as we discussed previously, is often used with minor transgressions, because dealing with the transgression might actually lead to a greater loss of face by self or others. *Humor*, while risky if used inappropriately, can be used to reframe transgressions and dissipate anger, particularly with relatively harmless infractions. In these situations, humor can actually acknowledge one's acceptance of blame, while demonstrating poise and social competence. *Apologies* also admit blame. However, full apologies typically include sincerity (nonverbal show of regret), a demonstration of understanding (why the behavior was hurtful), a plan as to how the offender will refrain from the offensive behavior in the future, restitution, and possibly a request for forgiveness. *Accounts* are explanations of one's actions that may include excuses and justifications. Excuses minimize one's responsibility for an event, whereas justifications attempt to reframe an event, often by minimizing the negative impact. *Aggression* is used at times when one feels embarrassed due to criticism, while *empathy* and *support* may be used to save face for a relational partner under the same circumstances. Finally, *physical remediation* is used in situations where a physical action can remedy the face-threatening situation (e.g., zipping up one's pants, cleaning up a mess).

Saving Face for Self and Others

Learning to manage one's own self successfully, and help keep others' face intact, is critical to successful relationship management and, in particular, walking through conflict productively. As we strive to create and maintain just relationships, we will find the pathway littered with obstacles if our, or our partners', face concerns become the central focus of the interaction. On the other hand, by intentionally working to maintain and save face for our partners (and, hopefully, our partners for us), we can *create spaces where if something good can happen, it will* (see Chapter Five: "Interpersonal Advocacy: Creating Spaces" for more on *creating space*).

Looking in the Mirror: Getting to Know Your Own Face

As we have started many chapters, we begin with self-awareness—how do you create your own face. Remember that face is the public identity, the sense of "self" (often our roles and unique, or favored, personal characteristics) we offer to others within specific relational contexts and interactions (Cupach & Metts, 1994). That means we may vary the face we present in different contexts, relationships, or even at different points of an interaction. In addition, because we are most aware of our face when it is threatened, we need to take time to understand what we perceive as most threatening to our face. For instance, research has indicated that embarrassing situations (e.g., social faux pas), mistakes, incompetence, relationship deterioration, and transgressions can all be face threatening (Cupach & Metts, 1994). If we hope to engage in interactions nondefensively, and without avoidance, it will help us to get to know our own face, and be keenly aware of those things to which we are most sensitive.

> *Living It Out: Think of two of your relationships, one that you perceive as somewhat conflictual or threatening, and one that is mostly peaceful. For each of these relationships, think about how you present yourself to the other person. What is similar, regarding your face, in these relationships? What is different?*
>
> *Living It Out: Now, think about the conflictual or threatening relationship. How and when do you feel your face threatened in this relationship? Think back to the section on facework and conflict. Is your initial response to the face-threatening behavior avoiding, dominating, or integrating? Do you typically have a secondary response that kicks in after your first response? In terms of maintaining your own identity and building a just relationship with your partner, do you consider these constructive or destructive responses?*

Saving Face for Others: Building and Protecting

Having a positive self-identity (e.g., self-esteem) is ultimately up to each person to create and maintain for him or herself, but as attentive relational partners seeking to create and maintain well-balanced relationships we can do our part to help build and protect our partner's face. Domenici and Littlejohn (2006) suggest a number of ways to build the face of others. *Honoring* is a means of showing others respect, such as using their title (e.g., "Miss," "Rabbi," "Dr."), complimenting them, or showing them praise. *Politeness* demonstrates respect to others, generally by adhering to culturally or relationally established norms. Interestingly, politeness takes into account the other person's need for autonomy and acceptance (Brown & Levinson, 1987; Domenici & Littlejohn, 2006). *Generosity* builds face by investing in others. This investment could take many forms, such as gifts, time, and service. Essentially, knowing you are worth someone else's investment builds your sense of self-worth. Finally, *support* shows another person that you value them. Support can take the form of listening, advice, approval, and affirmation.

We may also protect our relational partner's face. Again, Domenici and Littlejohn (2006) provide suggestions for this process. When we relay negative information in a way that is thoughtful and sensitive we are using *tact*. *Minimizing*, on the other hand, attempts to lessen the impact of a certain consequence, request, or obligation. For instance, "Sorry that you have to go to driver training school Saturday for your speeding ticket. But, I actually enjoyed it last time I went." Similarly, we found in our forgiveness research (Waldron & Kelley, 2008) that people often granted forgiveness by minimizing, in order to save face for their partner – "Don't worry about it, it was no big deal." *Avoidance* is a common way people protect the face of their partners. Again, in our forgiveness research with long-term couples, we found that partners avoided certain topics or details about events when we interviewed them together, as compared to when we interviewed them individually. Privately, they told us that when their spouse was present they withheld certain information to protect her or him. Finally, *prevention* is a proactive means of advising individuals regarding face-protection, "I would wait to tell her, she is stressed out right now," "If you go through with that, I don't think people will find it funny."

> *Living It Out: Think of one of your relationships in which face building could enhance or stabilize your relationship. How might you help build the face of your relationship partner this week? Be specific.*
>
> *Living It Out: Reflect on a time where one of your relational partners was embarrassed or defensive. How might you have been able to respond so that it would help them save face?*

Face and Dialogue

Face is a critical element of *just* interactions, because once we take things "personally" in an interaction, our attention shifts from problem-solving about the verbal topic to managing our own face. So face-saving is not just something "nice" to do for ourselves or for our partners, it is critical to establishing genuine dialogue with our partners. As long as we are busy protecting our public face, our persona (Tournier, 1957), we lose the benefits of genuine dialogue (see Chapter Three: "Good Relationships"). We must build and save face, for ourselves and for our relationship partners, because it is only when we are safe and secure in who we are (when we "feel good in our own skin") that we are willing to engage honestly and lovingly with one another, and thus, ensure a long-lasting justice in how we relate together.

> *Living It Out: Consider your own sense of self. How secure is it? Are you secure enough to engage honestly and lovingly with your relational partner? Are you secure enough to have genuine dialogue with your relationship partner? If not, how can you feel "good in your own skin"? ("Feeling good" can develop in many ways. Consider positive social connection, learned competencies, and spirituality. And, don't forget the suggestions in the previous section.)*
>
> *Living It Out: Consider your relationship partner. How secure is he or she? How might you help build or protect your partner's sense of self, so that the two of you might eventually engage in genuine dialogue? (Again, don't forget the suggestions in the previous section.)*

Case 8.1

Kat and Lydia are both genuinely nice people. In the workplace, they each manage major departments, are well liked by their colleagues, and are able to work through difficult issues with employees. However, simple conversations back at their apartment are nonproductive, at best, and often leave one or both of them with hurt feelings. Seemingly simple conversations go something like this:

Kat: How was your day?
Lydia: Pretty good. You? Anything interesting pop up?
Kat: Why do you always think that my work isn't interesting?
Lydia: I didn't say that. I was just trying to be polite.
Kat: So, you don't really want to know? It's just politeness like you would use with anyone at work?
Lydia: Okay, I quit! Every time I try to be nice to you, you accuse me of being insincere or manipulative. (*Lydia begins to leave*)
Kat: I didn't say that. I know you care about me, you just don't show it very well.
Lydia: You have issues. I'm out. (*leaves the room*)

Processing

1. Identify Kat's and Lydia's statements and actions that are avoiding, dominating, or integrating.
2. Rewrite this scenario, for Kat and Lydia, using face-building and face-protecting strategies.

Case 8.2

Next month, Carrie and John will have been dating for one year. They met through a mutual friend and things moved quickly, culminating with them moving in together after only knowing each other for one month. John loved Carrie's fun, outgoing personality. Before moving in together, he told her that he is totally committed to her and wants to take care of her. Carrie was drawn to John's strength of character. She knew he feels strongly about things and has a temper, but she also liked his strong feelings and, at times, she liked being "taken care of." However, a month after they moved in together, John "firmly" grabbed Carrie's arm during an argument. Later that day Carrie said something about his having grabbed her arm too hard, but John just told her that it was no big deal, and that he would "never, *ever*, hurt her." However, over time, acts of aggression became more common. During arguments John has put his hand through a wall, physically pulled new shoes off of Carrie's feet, and numerous times grabbed her forcibly about the shoulders when trying to get her to agree with him. Every time Carrie tries to talk to him about it, John denies that his being "physical" is inappropriate and shifts the blame back to her. Once when she mentioned he get counseling, John became furious, threw a kitchen chair across the room, and shouted, "I'm not going to counseling because of your problems!", and left the house.

Carrie is confused and doesn't know what to do. She loves John, but she is starting to wonder if she is physically and emotionally safe. A couple of her close friends have been telling her to get out, but she doesn't want to admit that she might have moved too quickly in this relationship. Even though John does not want to talk about his aggression, privately he is concerned. As a child he saw his dad hit his mom, but he doesn't want to admit that he is "turning into his dad."

Processing

1. How is face playing a role, for both John and Carrie, in this situation?
2. In what specific ways is John protecting his face?
3. How is facework inhibiting Carrie's and John's ability to dialogue with each other, and friends and family?
4. How might Carrie be able to build and protect John's face so that he could be more open to talking (dialogue) about his aggression?
5. How might Carrie's friends be able to build and protect Carrie's face so that she could be more open to talking (dialogue) about John's aggression?

References

Brown, P., & Levinson, S. (1987). *Politeness: Some universals in language usage.* Cambridge, UK: Cambridge University Press.

Burgoon, J. K., & Hale, J. L. (1984). The fundamental topoi of relational communication. *Communication Monographs, 51,* 193–214.

Canary, D. J., Cunningham, E. M., & Cody, M. J. (1988). Goal types, gender and locus of control in managing interpersonal conflict. *Communication Research, 15*, 426–446.

Cupach, W. R., & Metts, S. (1994). *Facework*. Thousand Oaks, CA: Sage.

Domenici, K., & Littlejohn, S. W. (2006). *Facework: Bridging theory and practice*. Thousand Oaks, CA: Sage.

Goffman, E. (1959). *Presentation of self in everyday life*. New York: Doubleday.

Knobloch, L. K., Satterlee, K. L., & DiDomenico, S. M. (2010). Relational uncertainty predicting appraisals of face threat in courtship: Integrating uncertainty reduction theory and politeness theory. *Communication Research, 37*(3), 303–334. doi: 0.1177/0093650210362527

Oetzel, J., Garcia, A. J., & Ting-Toomey, S. (2007). An analysis of the relationships between face concerns and facework behaviors in perceived conflict situations: A four-culture investigation. *International Journal of Conflict Management, 19*, 382–403.

Tournier, P. (1957). *The meaning of persons*. San Francisco: Harper & Row.

Waldron, V. R., & Kelley, D. L. (2008). *Communicating forgiveness*. Thousand Oaks, CA: Sage.

9

SHAME ON YOU, SHAME ON ME

"Devon, shame on you!" "Leanne, you are naughty. Shame!" "You should be ashamed of yourself! Go to your room this minute." Many of us heard these messages growing up. Perhaps we have said these same things to our own children, or pets, or even ourselves, with the positive intention of correcting "bad" behavior. Each of these statements is based on the idea that shame motivates people to correct behavior. And, you might be thinking, "Yes! If you've done something wrong you should feel badly about it." And, I agree. However, there is a difference between feeling badly about yourself, and feeling badly about something you've done.

I argue throughout this chapter that the act of blaming, especially when it involves shaming, frequently results in behavioral responses that inhibit the positive change we hope for. Consider my friend, Torrence, who told me a few months back that in a number of ways he felt deep shame about who he is. He blamed himself for certain poor personal decisions (he had betrayed a friend's confidence when he fell into financial troubles), and felt others' accusing stares. Interestingly, this internal sense of shame didn't result in changed behavior on his part. Rather, it often manifested itself in defensiveness, anger, and blaming others ("I did what I did because I was forced into this situation!"). He believed and espoused, "The best defense is a good offense" and "Do unto others before they do unto you." In other words, as we saw in the previous chapter on facework (Chapter 7: "Saving Face"), his shame led to protecting himself through aggression and control. And, when these strategies didn't seem to work, or were inappropriate, he simply withdrew from the situation and avoided.

In contrast, a few nights ago I hurt this same friend's feelings. This morning, before writing this chapter, I met with Torrence to tell him I was sorry that I hurt his feelings. I wasn't ashamed of myself for what I had said to him, however, I was sorry that I communicated my thoughts in a way that was hurtful to him. I apologized, and we talked about how I could have said things differently, and then talked about some of the ideas that I had brought out that night. What I experienced in this situation was guilt. I regretted a specific behavior (in this case a few statements I had made). The difference between what I experienced (feeling guilt about saying something that hurt my friend) and what I saw from my shame-full friend, Torrence, was that my guilt motivated me to engage my friend, restore the relationship (over a $30 breakfast!), and change my future behavior (I learned I could have said what I did privately to him), while his shame from a few months back resulted in continued defensiveness and withdrawal that was void of any real personal change. I want to emphasize that I'm not a better person than Torrence. We both care about others and try to live well. We both have great families and have good friends. However, my guilt response motivates me to engage others and focus on a positive future, whereas his shame response causes him to withdraw emotionally from others, either through control or avoidance.

This chapter explores how blame and shame are justice concepts that often create a distance between ourselves and others, and work against the eventual establishment of just relationships. I begin by looking at why we blame, and identify some of blame's typical outcomes. Then I conceptually distinguish between shame and guilt and highlight key behavioral responses. The chapter finishes by offering a model of *embracing responsibility*, as opposed to accepting blame, as a means of creating and restoring just and loving relationships.

Blame

Blaming creates, and reflects, a relationship frame that is often not useful in the creation and maintenance of just relationships. As we saw in Chapter Six: "Worldview: Your Relationship Frame," attributions are very much related to how we frame our relationships. Let's explore this more fully, in light of blame.

Attribution theory focuses on our need, as human beings, to make sense of our world—in essence, to ask, "Why?" (Manusov & Spitzberg, 2008). Why do things happen the way they do? What behavior results in certain outcomes? And, specifically, as it relates to our relationships, is someone to blame? When we are searching for meaning to a particular relational event we mentally process a number of possible reasons why the event occurred ("Did she slam the door because she was angry, or because her hands were full and she had to push it shut with her foot?").

Most central to the attribution process is determining how likely my partner's behavior is caused by internal or external factors—in other words, is my partner to blame for his action? Internal causation is dispositional—I attribute the cause of my partner's behavior to his personality. External causation is circumstantial—I see my partner's behavior as affected by environmental factors. Consider, for a moment, my friend Andrew. Andrew never had money when we would go out, always promised to pay the money back, but never did. You can tell by the way I have written this that I blame Andy for taking advantage of his friends. I see this as a personality characteristic—he was irresponsible and not thoughtful of his friends. However, Andy always cast the issue as externally caused—"An appointment went late, so I was running late and forgot my wallet," "When I changed pants, I left my wallet in the other pair," "My brother borrowed all my money." My assessment of Andy is related to two other factors, as well: is Andy's way of behaving stable or unstable (is it likely to stay this way and be repeated), and is it capable of being controlled (can Andy reasonably do something to change his behavior). One way of looking at this is we determine whether we think the other person is responsible for his past actions and whether or not we think he is capable of changing his behavior in the future (note that the latter is also part of how we humanize or dehumanize others; see Chapter Seven: "Dehumanizing the 'Other' "). This process is critical because it affects how we respond to the past and whether we have hope for constructing a just future together.

Interesting research with married couples illustrates the importance of the attribution process in marriage. The marriage relationship is an important relational context because it helps us understand the effects of relational attributions when there is a high level of interdependence in the relationship. Significant research by Bradbury and Fincham (1992) discovered that partners who held maladaptive attributions about their spouse also engaged in less productive problem-solving skills during marital interaction. And, they found that more distressed couples held more maladaptive causal attributions, the tendency to attribute marital problems to their partners and see them as global (occur across problem areas) and stable (likely to occur in the future). Distressed couples also held more maladaptive responsibility attributions, which involved blaming their partners and seeing their actions as intentional and selfish. Significantly, the effect of holding maladaptive attributions was associated with partners exhibiting interpersonally hostile and rejecting behavior. In addition, especially for wives, holding maladaptive responsibility attributions was associated with compromised problem-solving skills and being less likely to reciprocate their husbands' empathic and supportive behavior. The upshot of all this is that *blaming our partners may diminish our own ability to communicate constructively with them*.

As one would expect, blame also affects the one being blamed. Gottman's (1994) work focusing on marital communication patterns demonstrates that defensiveness and negative communication is often reciprocated by married partners, especially if they are somewhat unhappy in their relationship. Gottman (1994) tells us that, "The typical defensive statement is self-protective and avoidant of blame and responsibility" (p. 27). Defensiveness often takes on a tone of defensive whining, characterized by indignation and self-righteousness. This negativity, when reciprocated by partners, creates patterns of communication that inhibit positive communication and productive problem-solving. The bottom line is that blame affects the communication of the blamer and the one being blamed in such a way that it inhibits positive communication and the ability to create just, fair relationships.

Shame and Guilt

We have just discussed one common reaction to blame—defensiveness. However, blame generated from one's self or one's partner may also elicit feelings of guilt or shame. While our friends and family may somewhat commonly use the terms *guilt* and *shame* interchangeably ("I feel guilty that I didn't give Sabrina the $20 I owed her," "I'm so ashamed that I can't remember to pay back Sabrina."), researchers and practitioners distinguish between these concepts. Fisher and Exline (2010) identify guilt as an emotional response focused on a "specific wrong doing," whereas shame is an emotional response focused on one's "whole self" (p. 549). To expand on this distinction, consider, "Guilt is an other-oriented emotion that is linked to empathic and prosocial behavior" (p. 553), whereas, shame is an unpleasant negative emotion that is often experienced as feeling "small, worthless, and powerless" (p. 551). A critical distinction between guilt and shame is that guilt often leads to prosocial behavior that is other- or relationship-oriented ("I feel guilty because I understand that I hurt you"), whereas shame tends to be self-focused, engendering responses, such as defensiveness, withdrawal, or attack, to alleviate one's own discomfort.

An interesting study, focusing on divorce, found significant differences between individuals who felt guilty and those who felt shame (Wietzker, Buysse, Loeys, & Brondeel, 2011). In essence, the guiltier the divorcing participants felt, the less likely they were to force their position, instead tending to yield and problem-solve with their partners. On the other hand, the more shame participants felt, the more likely they were to avoid or use forceful communication during negotiations and the less likely they were to work toward constructive problem-solving. The implications of these findings are that guilt is related to openness and joint problem-solving (co-creating solutions), whereas shame is related to negative communication strategies, including avoiding any communication at all.

Choosing Responsibility Over Blame and Shame

Although many of us were raised in cultures that blamed and shamed as a way to achieve moral behavior or adherence to cultural norms ("Shame on you!"), the research just reviewed indicates that the blame→shame approach to relationships may actually work against achieving one's desired goals. As Fisher and Exline (2010) state, "Shame could lead offenders in a variety of unhelpful directions. Those experiencing shame might avoid facing their offenses, perhaps excusing them or behaving in aggressive or self-destructive ways. Alternatively, those experiencing shame could get caught up in self-condemning responses" (p. 552).

The restorative justice movement provides insight as to how we can reduce shame and, yet, increase personal responsibility and changed behavior. Listen to Dickey's (1998) eloquent description of restorative justice:

> Restorative justice defines justice as the restoration to wholeness of those whose lives and relationships have been broken or deeply strained by a criminal offense. This understanding of justice focuses on the harm the offense has caused to the victim, to the victim-offender relationship, and to the relationships of both the victim and the offender to the community. It asks: How can the harm be remedied? How can the victim's material loss be restored? How can the emotional trauma be healed? How can the relationship between the victim and offender, broken by the offense, be repaired?
>
> *(p. 107)*

Dickey highlights the restorative justice movement's focus on connection between offenders and victims. Through this process both sets of individuals begin to see the humanity of the other, often culminating with a plan for restitution. In this way, justice is *restorative* both in the sense of restoring the humanity of both offender and offended, and restoring the more tangible elements of their life situations (e.g., repaying funds, painting a building that was tagged with graffiti, creating a program to educate people about domestic violence). Restorative justice does not necessarily seek a full, extended reconciliation between individuals, but it does bring both sides together to embrace their humanity and create a just future for both parties (even if that future is separate from one another).

To pull this all together, shame is feeling badly about one's whole self (as opposed to feeling badly about specific behaviors), often resulting in anti-social and self-destructive behavior. In essence, shame isolates, often diminishing the possibility of achieving

---

IT'S NOT ME

By Shanae G.

From my heart
From my soul
From my mind
From the drama
To my love
From my kids
From this to that
From the man above
From this
I have learned to expect this
Take this pain that follows me
And speak from my heart
Speak from my brain
Allow no shame or give no blame
it's not the same
I've changed
I speak with authority
I live with peace
I admire smiles and fix frowns
I just want to succeed
I just want to be me and not what you're used to seeing.

My perceptions: I started to pay more attention to myself and why certain things would happen to me. I noticed that pain is not only caused by an individual but can be caused by you, yourself. So, if I have the ability to recognize my emotions and what triggers the pain, I have the ability to move forward.

changed relationships and behavior. In contrast, guilt is conceptualized as feeling positively about one's whole self, yet badly about a negative behavior for which one is responsible. Feeling positively about one's self provides a foundation to act in prosocial ways, and feeling guilty about one's behavior provides the motivation to restore one's relationship. Thus, the path to just and fair relationships comes not by shaming others, but by affirming others and letting them take responsibility for their own actions.

Building Shame-Less Relationships

As we have seen, blaming and shaming often inhibit the ability to create loving, just relationships. In fact, instead of building positive relationships, they may actually create emotional distance between partners as individuals become defensive, and attack or withdraw from situations and one another. An alternative approach is to decrease shame for our partners and ourselves, and create relationship-enhancing attributions (rather than distress-maintaining attributions) that create a supportive environment for dialogue and problem-solving.

Relationship-Enhancing Attributions

We have seen some of the potential downsides to blaming in contrast to helping others take responsibility for their actions. We know that negative internal, stable, and global attributions can inhibit our desire to work with others on relationship problems. Essentially, when I begin blaming, "This is just the way she is. She will never change," it creates a hopelessness that there is no use working together. Seeking additional information about a person or situation, when it is done to facilitate understanding, can begin to change our relational frame from distress-maintaining to relationship-enhancing—"I know she means well and that she's been under a lot of pressure. Maybe we can work together to create a better solution to our problem." Our previous discussions regarding mindfulness (nonjudgmental awareness) and imaginative empathy can move us from blaming and shaming to taking responsibility and jointly creating constructive responses.

> *Living It Out: Do you blame people to try to motivate change? How might you change the attributions you make about others so that they are relationship-enhancing?*
>
> *Living It Out: Rather than trying to force change through blaming and shaming others, what if you were to create an environment "where if something good can happen, it will"? (see Chapter Five: "Interpersonal Advocacy"). How might you communicate to others that you believe they are valuable and want to work with them to solve your shared problems?*

Decreasing Shame while Increasing Responsibility

Fisher and Exline (2010) suggest the following shame-reducing strategies gleaned from the restorative justice movement:

Restorative justice emphasizes the development of empathy, personal responsibility, and a sense of control, all while working to reduce the offender's shame-based identity as a bad person. . . . Offenders are taught to distinguish between themselves and their actions, learning to accept that doing bad things does not necessarily mark them as bad people.

(p. 552)

In addition, Fisher and Exline suggest that education distinguishing between shame and guilt can be helpful, as well as adopting a transcendent sense of humility, self-compassion, and self-acceptance. This process is characterized by the willingness to take an honest look, without judgment (think mindfulness), at one's own strengths and weaknesses, and to reconnect to others through taking responsibility for one's own actions. Often the development of rituals helps individuals abandon their self-shame and embrace a new sense of positive identity. For example, certain jails and prisons have created reading programs for inmates and their children, such that both parent and child are reading the same books and able to discuss them during regular phone contact. Through programs such as this, inmates may begin to release the shame of having abandoned their children while incarcerated, and instead embrace a new image of "good parent" as they read with their children.

> *Living It Out: Think about something for which you feel shame. Take a moment to distinguish between what you did and who you are. Now, turn shame on its head— the very fact that you feel shame indicates that your heart is good, and you have the freedom to turn your shame (feeling badly about yourself) into guilt (feeling badly about something you've done). Take the guilt that you've exchanged for shame, and think about what you can do to make things "right" with the person you offended.*
> *Living It Out: Privately, write down something for which you feel shame. Now, make a list of at least three good qualities you hold (e.g.," I care about people," "I love my children," "I am organized."). Put this list in your phone's notepad or handwrite it and put it in your purse or wallet as a constant reminder that you are valuable.*
> *Living It Out: Like the reading program for inmates and their children, create a ritual that serves as a reminder of your positive identity and connects you in positive ways to others. (Many find meditation or times of silent prayer as beneficial rituals.)*

Shame Resilience

Bestselling author and researcher Brene Brown (2012) suggests that resistance to shame is impossible. As long as we care about connection with others we will experience some level of shame at various points in our lives. Instead, her research demonstrates that individuals who productively manage shame are *shame resilient*. The key to being shame resilient? Empathy. As Brown (2012) states, "If we can share our story with someone who responds with empathy and understanding, shame can't survive" (p. 75). She suggests four elements that lead us to shame resilience and empathy. First, recognize when you are experiencing shame and what triggers it. Second, become critically aware of the messages and expectations that drive your shame. Are these true and reasonable? Third, reach out. This is difficult for many of us, because we're already hurting. We want affirmation from others, but we remain hidden and they don't know what is really happening in our lives. We must reach out. We must commit to staying connected to safe others. Finally, Brown tells us to speak shame. By this she means that it is important to let others know what you are feeling and what you need from them.

> *Living It Out: Take a few minutes to assess your experience of shame. Do you know when you are experiencing shame? Are you able to identify what most often triggers shame for you? What does shame feel like to you? What is your "natural" response to feeling ashamed?*
>
> *Living It Out: The tendency of shame-full people is to isolate. Make a plan for how you can stay connected to others when you feel ashamed. For example, who can you safely talk to? How can you tell them what you need? Let empathetic others inside your experience!*

Case 9.1

Barrett had always been a great kid. He did well in school and was vice president of his class in his junior year of high school. He grew up in a loving family that held very strict rules about the children's behavior—you're grounded if you're late for curfew (even if you're late by one minute—just don't be late!), absolutely no drinking until you are 21 (that includes "tastes" of parents' drinks), you are never to be alone with someone of the opposite sex. Barrett adhered to these rules and believed his parents established them "for his own good."

One night Barrett was at a friend's house. Unbeknownst to him, the friend's parents were out of town and a few other friends came over with alcohol. Because Barrett's friends knew that he didn't drink, they thought it would be funny to get him drunk—which they did. As the party wrapped up, Barrett was dropped off at his house by a friend, before curfew. He said a quick "Hi" to his parents, said he wasn't feeling well, and went straight to bed. The next morning he vaguely remembered that at the party, he and a girl he had a crush on (Jamie) had had sex in a back bedroom.

Barrett experienced a great deal of shame about getting drunk and having sex. He had always prided himself on following the rules, respecting his parents, and being a good student. Truth be told, he had seen himself as a role model for some of the "wilder" kids at school, but now he felt worse than his friends because he had violated his own moral code. It took weeks for Barrett to stop feeling like a failure and a fraud. He even thought he should resign from the student council. During this time friends and family kept asking Barrett if he was okay—he just didn't seem to be himself. Then, six weeks after the party, Jamie told him she was pregnant, and that it had to be his. This sent Barrett into an emotional spiral of shame and fear. After two weeks of confusion, panic, and depression, Barrett went to his youth group leader and talked it out. The leader assured Barrett that he wasn't a "bad" person for what he'd done. He eventually helped Barrett and Jamie make a plan for how they could, together, tell each of their parents what had happened. Here are their parents' responses:

Jamie's Parents:	"Jamie, we trusted you. And, Barrett, we're so disappointed. We thought you were a good young man. Now we see that you're just like all the other boys. You just use girls and get away without any of the real consequences."
Barrett's Parents:	"Barrett, you know you've broken our trust, and there will be consequences for your actions. But this just isn't like you. Can you tell us how this happened? You both must be scared to death."

Processing

1. Early in the story when Barrett first remembered what happened at the party, was he experiencing shame or guilt? How does your answer clarify why Barrett responded as he did?
2. Think about Brene Brown's recommendations to be shame resilient. How did sharing his story with his youth leader help Barrett become shame resilient? How did Barrett's youth group leader's response help turn Barrett's emotional experience from shame to guilt?
3. Using attribution theory and the conceptual distinctions between blame, shame, and guilt, discuss the differences between each set of parents' responses.

Case 9.2

Jessica is a senior at college, and proud to be a first-generation student. She is a United States citizen, but was raised in a household where Spanish was the primary language spoken. She will be her family's first college graduate. With a lot of hard work she has managed to get her English language skills to a level where she regularly scores B-grades on her papers for class, and she has even thought about graduate school.

Jessica has been with the same boyfriend, Carlos, since her senior year in high school. During her freshman year, to save money, she and Carlos moved in together. Carlos is undocumented because his parents brought him to this country when he was just 2 years old. He was an average student in high school and unable to go to college because of the cost. However, he works hard for a local construction crew.

Jessica has had an uphill battle to climb. She used to feel like she was "stupid," and unable to do basic things that seemed to come to others so easily (like manage a bank account). Also, her mother loves her, but has never understood her desire to go to college: "Quit trying to be something you're not. Being a mom was enough for me, why can't it be enough for you?" As such, college has complicated her life in many ways. She has discovered that she really is smart and some of the problems she had before were mostly because of cultural differences (e.g., she once missed a multiple choice question on an exam because she didn't know what a casserole was). In her sophomore year she began telling her story to her college professors—in response, many of them empathized with her experience and helped her stay positive ("I really am smart," "I can do this!"). She actually started each day by looking at a note she posted on her bathroom mirror—"You are worth it!"

Her college career has also contributed to problems in her relationship with Carlos. He agrees with her mother that she should stay home and they should build a family. However, as time has gone on, instead of talking with her about this issue, Carlos has withdrawn. Jessica sums up their problems as follows:

> I think Carlos is glad for my success, but also threatened by it. He feels badly about himself because his English is not that good and he can only get laborer jobs, whereas I am now in an internship with a public relations firm. I still love Carlos, but it seems like he has pulled away from me. When we are together, we end up arguing (it usually starts by him blaming me for being "too good" for him), and then he goes to hang out with his friends. I'm just not sure he is capable of change. I don't know what's going to happen with us.

Processing

1. How is Jessica and Carlos's experience of shame affected by their upbringing?
2. How has Jessica learned to practice shame resilience?
3. How is Carlos's experience of shame affecting his ability to work things out with Jessica?

References

Bradbury, T. N., & Fincham, F. D. (1992). Attributions and behavior in marital interaction. *Journal of Personality and Social Psychology, 63*, 613–628.

Brown, B. (2012). *Daring greatly: How the courage to be vulnerable transforms the way we live, love, parent, and lead.* New York: Gotham Books.

Dickey, W. J. (1998). Forgiveness and crime: The possibilities of restorative justice. In R. D. Enright & J. North (Eds.), *Exploring forgiveness* (pp. 106–120). Madison, WI, USA: The University of Wisconsin Press.

Fisher, M. L., & Exline, J. J. (2010). Moving toward self-forgiveness: Removing barriers related to shame, guilt, and regret. *Social and Personality Psychology Compass, 4*(8), 548–558.

Gottman, J. M. (1994). *What predicts divorce? The relationship between marital processes and marital outcomes.* Hillsdale, NJ: Lawrence Erlbaum.

Manusov, V., & Spitzberg, B. (2008). Attribution theory: Finding good cause in the search for theory. In L. A. Baxter & D. O. Braithwaite (Eds.), *Engaging theories in interpersonal communication: Multiple perspectives* (pp. 37–49). Los Angeles: Sage.

Wietzker, A., Buysse, A., Loeys, T., & Brondeel, R. (2011). Easing the conscience: Feeling guilty makes people cooperate in divorce negotiations. *Journal of Social and Personal Relationships, 29*, 324–336.

PART III

Shaping Just Relationships

Creating a Just Future

10

RESILIENCE

Ordinary Magic

In the classic film *A Streetcar Named Desire*, Blanche cries out, "I don't want reality, I want magic!" After watching the film, Blanche's words haunted me—I want magic, too. I've always loved magic. However, for both Blanche and me, our pursuit of magic hasn't always been healthy. Perhaps that is why Ann Masten's (2001) article, *Ordinary Magic*, had such an effect on me. Masten writes about resilience in children. She is combating the idea that at-risk children who survive are somehow extraordinary. Instead, she proposes the concept of "ordinary magic." Masten states that, "The most surprising conclusion emerging from studies of these [at-risk] children is the ordinariness of resilience" (p. 227). Masten's perspective gives us hope.

Resiliency is our natural state. When we act in resilient ways, we are tapping into our ordinary magic. As we cultivate a resilient sense of self, and learn to communicate in ways that create resilient relationships, we are *creating spaces where if something good can happen, it will*. Specifically, we are creating resilience spaces where just relationships are possible. Resilient people are secure in who they are and the basic possibilities of their relationships, even when their circumstances look grim. Following, I overview the basic concept of resilience with specific attention to characteristics of resilient children and youth. I then examine how we create resilience in our relationships, focusing on characteristics of resilient families. As always, the chapter finishes with specific ideas as to how we might begin *Living It Out*.

Resilience

Masten (2001) defines resilience as "a class of phenomena characterized by good outcomes in spite of serious threats to adaptation or development" (p. 228). In other words, when my first-generation students overcome financial struggles to attend university—resilience. When single moms work long hours, yet raise healthy children (like my mom did!)—resilience. When low-income students rise above poorly equipped schools, and family conditions ill-suited to studying, and become valedictorian—resilience.

Masten's definition highlights two basic assumptions important to understanding how resilience works in our lives. First, we do experience positive functioning and good outcomes in our lives, in spite of the fact that we incur threats to our viability. Second, the natural human condition is one characterized by growth and adaptation to a changing environment. The first assumption calls us to understand risks to our viability, and protective factors that minimize those risks. The second assumption points us to those things that keep us adaptable and growing.

Risks can be understood as "events, conditions, or experiences that increase the probability, but do not ensure, that a problem will be formed, maintained, or exacerbated" (Anthony, Alter, & Jenson, 2009, p. 46). Risk for children and adults can include environmental (poverty, lack of resources, neighborhood and school deficits), interpersonal/social (poor parent-child bonding, school failure, association with negative peers, family substance abuse), and individual factors (poor impulse control, family history of alcoholism, learning or personality disorders) (Anthony et al., 2009; Lucas & Buzzanell, 2012). Most simply put, when the odds of success are lower than "normal," you are at risk. Or, reframed, resilience is attributed to those who "beat the odds" (Schoon, 2006).

Protective or promotive factors minimize or buffer the potential effects of risk and stressors on various life outcomes (Beck & Socha, 2015). Like risk, they can be viewed as environmental (educational and career opportunities, social support from nonfamily members), interpersonal/social (attachment to parents, low parental conflict, caring relationships with siblings), and individual (positive attitude, problem solving skills) (Anthony et al., 2009). Protective factors, or what have also been called "developmental assets" (Richardson, 2002, p. 309), can include any of the following: being robust, socially responsible, adaptable, mindful, achievement oriented, humorous, female, and a good communicator; and having self-efficacy, the ability to regulate emotion, a close personal relationship with an adult (or other social support), and an internal locus of control (Beck & Socha, 2015; Richardson, 2002). These assets are useful starting points as we ask ourselves, "What characteristics help me bounce back?"

We have been focusing on the first resilience assumption regarding risk and protection as factors that determine our ability to achieve positive functioning and good outcomes in the face of threats to our viability. The second assumption draws attention to our ability as humans to adapt and grow. A central element of our humanity is our ability to adapt to our environment and change (Oelofsen, 2009, see Chapter Seven: "Dehumanizing the 'Other'"). Richardson (2002) describes this aspect of resilience, as follows:

> A succinct statement of resilience theory is that there is a force within everyone that drives them to seek self-actualization, altruism, wisdom, and harmony with a spiritual source of strength. This force is resilience. . . . The resiliency

movement is representative of how an interdisciplinary exchange and inquiry can help understand where and how we can access the motivation and drive to grow through adversity.

(p. 313)

Richardson goes on to suggest that it is useful for counselors and therapists (and may I suggest, relational partners?) to understand where a client's primary motivation is seated. Resilience is ecological in the sense that it is embedded in one's own relational or cultural context (Beck & Socha, 2015). As such, a person's motivation to adapt, change, and grow is embedded deep within her or his worldview, and can be conceptualized as chi, prana, spirit, God, or self-actualization. Practically, that means that some people are motivated to move forward because they see themselves as part of a bigger picture, or God's plan, or because they still hear their grandfather's voice encouraging them to, "Always get back up when you've been knocked down." This sense of connectedness to one's social environment moves us to take a closer look at the relational aspects of resilience. As Beck and Socha (2015) put it, "the need and place for human connection knows no limits" (p. 10).

Communicating Resilience

Extending Richardson's work, Buzzanell devises a communication approach to resilience by focusing on how individuals use everyday messages and stories to make meaning as they work toward "reintegrating from disruptions in life" (Buzzanell, 2010, p. 2; Lucas & Buzzanell, 2012). Her message and story-based approach takes Richardson's terminology and fleshes it out. To this end, she paints a picture of resilience as a process that is "dynamic, integrated, unfolding over time and through events, evolving into patterns and dependent on contingencies" (Buzzanell, 2010, p. 2). She identifies five communication-based processes that are central to creating resilient persons and relationships (Buzzanell, 2010): 1) crafting normalcy, 2) affirming identity anchors, 3) maintaining and using communication networks, 4) putting alternative logics to work, and 5) legitimizing negative feelings while foregrounding productive action.

Crafting normalcy represents attempts by individuals and family to return to living normally as soon as possible. Often this process is represented by the mundane—as I state elsewhere, "Daily interaction is the mortar between the bricks" (Kelley, 2012, p. 26). When disruption occurs, it is often the "little things" that keep us resilient, such as still going out to dinner on family night, getting your morning coffee, or having people over to watch "the game." Interestingly, Waldron and I (2008) found that people often forgive by "returning to normal," in an effort to avoid the past and move toward the future.

Affirming identity anchors references discourse that is intended to keep one's private identity or public face intact (see Chapter Eight: "Saving Face"). In Buzzanell and Turner's (2003) study of job loss, family members would protect the father's face through discourse that continued to reference dad as the breadwinner, household head, and decision maker. Typically, individuals reference their family, relational history, or family values to maintain identity in turbulent times. For example, an unexpected pregnancy at age 17 could be viewed in light of a family heritage of early pregnancies ("My mom was pregnant at age 17 and we have a great family.") It is important to acknowledge that while identity anchors may help stabilize individuals and families during disruption, they may also undercut necessary adaptation that is critical to resilience. Buzzanell and Turner (2003) found in certain families that when the husband lost his job, even though the wife or other family members were bringing in the majority of the income, this contribution could not be fully realized without undercutting the husband's identity.

Maintaining and using communication networks often discriminates between those who successfully adapt over time and those who are unable to maintain consistent change. Numerous family scholars have recognized that unhealthy families fail to maintain positive, realistic connections with their environments. For example, low-income families that move frequently often struggle to stay in contact with school systems, making it difficult for children to transition smoothly in their education. After divorce, single mothers may isolate themselves and their children in an effort to stabilize the new family structure, while actually undercutting their ability to adapt to their new environment. Consistent with these effects, lack of social support has been identified as a predictor of PTSD (posttraumatic stress disorder) responses (Bonanno, 2004).

Putting alternative logics to work is essentially learning to reframe situations or, as we discussed in Chapter Six: "Worldview: Your Relationship Frame," create a new relational frame through which to view persons, situations, and relationships. This process occurs in various ways. A common manifestation is when we reframe a situation, from disruption to opportunity—"Being laid-off is actually good for me, because I've been wanting to change careers." Also, related to attribution theory, we may reframe a situation as externally caused ("No one could have succeeded given the circumstances") in order to save face (protect our identity anchors). Another expression is to change negative relationship labeling into positive relationship labeling—consider how the following message reframes the idea of "family" during a fairly amicable divorce, "I know everyone is confused and anxious as your mom and I are divorcing. And that's okay. But, we want you to know that we are still a family, we are just going to do family in a new way."

Finally, legitimizing negative feelings while foregrounding productive action allows us to experience the full range of our emotional responses, without being debilitated by them. As we discussed in Chapter Seven: "Dehumanizing the 'Other,'" experiencing a complex range of emotions is part of what makes us human. It is essential that we develop hope through the experience of our emotions, while eventually being able to plan and move toward a just future (Beck & Socha, 2015). As I discuss in Chapter Twelve: "Forgiveness," moving forward in a healthy way requires processing one's emotional response to disruption or transgression. If we don't stay stuck in endless cycles of rumination, this is a healthy pathway to creating a productive future. For example, it is important to experience an emotional blend of anger, hurt, betrayal, confusion, and even love when you find out that your girlfriend had lunch with her ex-boyfriend without telling you. However, ruminating on the negative emotions can eventually ruin a salvageable relationship. Instead, learning from your emotions can tell you something about who you are and what you value. It can provide motivation and insight into the talk you are going to have with her later that night.

Building Resilient Persons and Relationships

To create just, fair, loving relationships we must become resilient people, and together build resilient relationships. Psychologist Scott Peck (1978) begins his classic book, *The Road Less Traveled*, with the following statement, "Life is difficult." According to Peck, neuroses are the result of our attempts to avoid legitimate suffering. When we change our relationship frame from one that says, "Life should work according to my plan" to "Life is often hard. When it's not hard, Woohoo! that's the icing on the cake," it builds a resilient framework with which to view life. As Presidential Medal of Freedom winner Isabel Allende (2014) stated, at age 71, "I train [for life] by saying 'Yes,' to whatever comes my way—drama, comedy, tragedy, love, death, losses. Yes, to life!"

Assessing Your Risk

A central element to creating and maintaining resilient, just relationships is to understand one's own risk, and potential for risk. Risk can be any choice that creates the likelihood of persistent problems for you, your partner, or your relationship. To the extent that each partner understands her or his "triggers," it becomes possible to proactively create protective factors. As I discuss in the next chapter, conflict and stress are often predictable. That works to our advantage in being ready to respond to triggers that put us at risk. In addition, knowing our personal triggers, having awareness of environmental elements that can create traumatic conditions, allows us to be proactive.

> *Living It Out: Are you currently at risk? Are their traumatic factors in your life that are compromising your ability to adapt and respond in productive ways? On a scale of one to ten, assess your own, and your partner's, current level of risk. Have your partner do the same and, together, discuss your risk level or differences in your perceptions of risk.*
>
> *Living It Out: Make a list of triggers that may put you at risk (two of my own risk factors are being too busy and feeling financial pressure). Next, identify environmental conditions that affect you negatively (e.g., the economy, work conditions, in-laws).*

Assessing Your Protective Factors

Protective factors are those elements that, when in place, minimize the potential effects of risk. These safeguards can be individual, interpersonal/relational, or environmental. And, while these safeguards are not completely under our individual control, we can learn to make choices that optimize the potential of these factors. Individual factors include personal characteristics, such as a strong self-esteem, specific skills (communication and problem-solving), high motivation, and a positive attitude. Interpersonal/relational factors include elements like having caring relationships, patterns of constructive conflict with relationship partners, and good social support. Environmental factors include positive job and school settings/opportunities, positive economic outlook in one's community, home/living environment, and useful resources and support from one's community.

> *Living It Out: Make a list of your individual, relational, and environmental protective factors.*
>
> *Living It Out: Compare your list of protective factors with your previous list of risks. How do these lists compare? Based on this comparison, how would you rate your potential for resilience?*
>
> *Living It Out: If you have weak areas of protection (protective factors), are there choices and actions you can make to strengthen each area?*

Communication That Enables Adaptability and Change

As we discussed previously, Buzzanell identifies five communication-based processes that facilitate resilience: 1) crafting normalcy, 2) affirming identity anchors, 3) maintaining and using communication networks, 4) putting alternative logics to work, and 5) legitimizing negative feelings while foregrounding productive action (Buzzanell, 2010; Lucas & Buzzanell, 2012). Each of these processes is managed, in part, within our personal relationships. Maintaining some type of normalcy and consistent identity provides stability during disruption. Keeping open communication with others enables us to adapt in constructive ways to our changing environment. Finally, allowing ourselves to process our emotional experience and reframe our thinking facilitates the creation of a constructive, hopeful, just future for ourselves and others.

> *Living It Out: Take time for your partner and you, individually, to think through each of the five communication-based processes that facilitate resilience. For each one, write down an example of how you have been resilient in the past (if you don't have a good example for one or more of these, don't worry, that's very typical). Next, share your lists and stories with one another. Finally, go through your lists and discuss how you can work together to strengthen each area (e.g., when my wife and I are stressed, keeping the house clean is one way I can help her feel a sense of normalcy in our lives).*

Case 10.1

Nicole has decided to move to Berkeley, California. She currently lives in Tulsa, Oklahoma, where she was born, but she is not close with her parents and Tulsa holds a lot of "bad" memories for her. So, she's decided to move. She's planning on living with her brother who is in graduate school at UC Berkeley and is pretty nervous about her decision. At 11 p.m. she sends a short text to her best friend Carmen. Thirty minutes later, the two of them are sitting at a local, late-night coffee bar.

Carmen: Wow, I knew you were unsettled, but I didn't know you were this unsettled.

Nicole: Yeah. It's kind of taken me by surprise, too.

Carmen: So tell me, why now? And, how serious are you? I mean, I don't want to make you mad, but you do kind of react too quickly sometimes and then later regret your decision.

Nicole: I know, that's why I wanted to talk to you. If I'm going to do this, it needs to be for the right reasons. You're right, I do overreact sometimes, but actually right now I'm doing pretty well. That's the weird thing. I feel like I could stay here, but I just don't want to. Like, if I'm going to make a move, this is the time.

Carmen: How much of this is about getting away from your parents?

Nicole: Some, but I've set pretty good boundaries with them so I hardly see them. I just think there are so many memories here that I'm not sure I can ever really figure out who I am, or who I can be, or whatever!

Carmen: I get that. I mean, I love you to death, but it's even frustrating for me to watch your life. You have so many great qualities, and yet I just keep waiting for you to see that, too! What about living with your brother? Haven't you been pretty frustrated with him?

Nicole: Absolutely. But I've decided to ask him if we can work on things. I am actually going to send him an email apologizing for some of the immature things I said to him in the past and asking if we can move on.

Carmen: I'm impressed. I wish I could do that with my sister. I just don't have the guts.

Nicole: Yeah, well, that's why I wanted to see you. I need you. Like, I need you now, to check in with . . . you know? Maybe I'll have you read the email to my brother before I send it. But, I'm really going to need your support after I move. I know things aren't always going to go smoothly.

Carmen: You know you've got it! I'll always be here for you. Hey, what if we each get a little "c" for courage tattooed on our wrists as a reminder of our friendship and to keep doing what we need to do?

Nicole: Awesome! You are THE BEST!

Processing

1. Identify three potential risk factors for Nicole.
2. What preventive factors were present, or not present, in Nicole and Carmen's discussion?
3. Using Buzzanell's five communication-based processes for resilience, assess how Carmen and Nicole were resilient, or planning for resilience, as they made decisions regarding Nicole's possible move.

Case 10.2

Sandra Hassan had been a middle school teacher for ten years in the Jefferson School District. After watching a documentary on inner-city education, Sandra requested that she be moved to an urban school, Dawson Butte Elementary, where over one-third of the students are under poverty level and one-half are considered at-risk (e.g., few family resources, and patterns of teen pregnancy, substance abuse, dropping out of school, and/or incarceration of family members). Two weeks after beginning teaching at Dawson Butte, Sandra began noticing Terresita (Terri).

Terri was in eighth grade—bright, highly motivated, and had a positive attitude. However, Sandra quickly became aware that in spite of these positive characteristics, Terri was often late with her homework and, a little too frequently, missed class altogether. Sandra also noticed that, in spite of her positive attitude, Terri often seemed tired or distracted. One day when the class was released for lunch, Sandra asked Terri to stay behind. Terri stayed, but looked uncomfortable with having been singled out. After some general conversation about school, Sandra asked Terri about life at home. Terri was the oldest of five siblings. She loved her mom, but eventually revealed that her mom sometimes used "too many drugs" or "too much alcohol," so sometimes she (Terri) stayed home to take care of her brothers and sisters. She also watched her siblings after school so she couldn't be on the softball team or, often, find time to get her homework finished.

This was all new to Sandra. She told Terri that she (Sandra) was always available to talk, if she wanted. She also said she'd be willing to talk to Mom, but Terri quickly said "No, thank you" to that. Sandra then told Terri, "I'm glad to let you turn assignments in late. You just need to tell me what's going on. Okay?" Terri teared up and, quietly, replied, "Yes." Sandra told her, "It's okay to feel sad, at times. And, I promise I won't ask too often about what's going on. I'll treat you like all the other kids. You're so wonderfully bright, you're going to make it through this."

Processing

1. What are the risk factors in Terri's life?
2. What elements have, thus far, protected Terri from succumbing to these risks?
3. What communication-based resilience processes have kept Terri functional? Which new ones has Sandra introduced into Terri's life?

References

Allende, I. (2014). How to live passionately—no matter your age. https://www.ted.com/talks/isabelle_allende_how_to_live_passionately_no_matter_your_age?language=en

Anthony, E. K., Alter, C. F., & Jenson, J. M. (2009). Development of a risk and resilience-based out-of-school time program for children and youths. *Social Work, 54*, 45–55.

Beck, G. A., & Socha, T. (2015). *Communicating home and resilience across the lifespan.* New York: Peter Lang.

Bonanno, G. A. (2004). Loss, trauma, and human resilience: Have we underestimated the human capacity to thrive after extremely aversive events? *American Psychologist, 59*, 20–28.

Buzzanell, P. M. (2010). Resilience: Talking, resisting, and imagining new normalcies into being. *Journal of Communication, 60*, 1–14.

Buzzanell, P. M., & Turner, L. H. (2003). Emotion work revealed by job loss discourse: Backgrounding-foregrounding of feelings, construction of normalcy, and (re)instituting of traditional masculinities. *Journal of Applied Communication Research, 31*, 27–57.

Kelley, D. L. (2012). *Marital communication.* Cambridge: Polity Press.

Lucas, K., & Buzzanell, P. M. (2012). Memorable messages of hard times: Constructing short- and long-term resiliencies through family communication. *Journal of Family Communication, 12*, 189–208.

Masten, A. S. (2001). Ordinary magic: Resilience processes in development. *American Psychologist, 56*, 227–238.

Oelofsen, R. (2009). De- and rehumanization in the wake of atrocities. *South African Journal of Philosophy, 28*(2), 178–188.

Peck, S. (1978). *The road less traveled.* New York: Touchstone.

Richardson, G. E. (2002). The metatheory of resilience and resiliency. *Journal of Clinical Psychology, 58*, 307–321.

Schoon, I. (2006). *Risk and resilience: Adaptations in changing times.* Cambridge: Cambridge University Press.

Waldron, V. R., & Kelley, D. L. (2008). *Communicating forgiveness.* Thousand Oaks, CA: Sage.

11

ENGAGING CONFLICT

Learning to Balance Power

Engaging conflict is a process. It is choosing to enter into conflict, to become interlocked, not to avoid. As we discussed regarding resilience, it is to say, "Yes, to what comes your way" (Allende, 2014). But, engaging conflict is also a description of the type of conflict we create—it is conflict that grabs our attention, that attracts and holds fast, that even pleases. Engaging conflict is conflict that engages our whole, healthy selves.

Engaging conflict is essential to creating just relationships. *Social justice* brings conflict to life. When we speak of social justice, it is generally because we, or those we care about, are experiencing a lack of equity or balance—when we experience life as unfair. Yet, attempting to restore balance is often met with resistance. This chapter on conflict concentrates on the restoration of balance to relationships. I begin by looking at relationship systems as resistant to change, emphasizing how mindless behavior patterns can be a form of resistance. I then focus on two critical aspects of managing conflict. First, I examine the management of arousal processes as a means of staying focused in the present and creating just process. Second, I examine types of meaning that are embedded in conflict messages and explore how engaging conflict creates an opportunity to balance power in relationships. I finish this section by offering the concept of transcendent discourse, as a means to process moral conflict and create genuine dialogue.

Relational Systems and Mindless Resistance to Change

Families, communities, even friends and couples are systems in and of themselves. Simply put, a system is any interdependent set of objects. If we take Desmond Tutu's (1999) perspective on Ubuntu (see Chapter Four: "Love Relationships"), the very nature of being human is to be embedded in various systems, to be interdependent with others. In essence, we exist within relational systems.

For our purposes here, I want to focus on a characteristic common to all forms of human systems—resistance to change. Systems theorists refer to this as *homeostasis* (Watzlawick, Beavin, & Jackson, 1967). Homeostasis is a survival mechanism. It restricts change and maintains the status quo in an effort to sustain the system's viability—much like the human body works to maintain a temperature of approximately 98.6 degrees. Homeostasis within human relationships manifests itself by restricting change in communication patterns, roles, and balancing power. For example, no matter your age, when you go to your parents' house for Thanksgiving and your Mom says, "Wipe your feet before coming in," you may do so automatically, because it is what you know. This is how you and your mom know how to relate to one another—mother-child. Unconsciously she communicates to you in ways that feel natural to her, and you respond in like kind. However, to survive, systems must also adapt to changing environments (Galvin, Dickson, & Marrow, 2006). This process has been referred to as *morphogenesis*. To use the preceding example, morphogenesis occurs when you hear mother follow up her foot wiping statement with something like, "I hear you've become quite an editor at work. I could use your help, later today, with a document I have to send to my production team Monday morning." This shift in traditional roles (Mom asking for help on a task for her workplace) may represent a healthy adaptation. In essence, systems need a balance between stability and change in order to survive.

A cognitive process that facilitates homeostasis is *mindlessness* (Langer, 1989). Mindlessness is unconscious, automated patterns of behaving and thinking (Kelley, 2012). As such, mindless responses are based on past information and experience (Burpee & Langer, 2005; Kellermann, 1992). These automatic reactions allow for quick, efficient responses to external stimuli. For example, in the preceding example with Mom, her "wipe your feet" comment probably came out mindlessly, without much conscious thought. Her quick reaction upon your arrival is based on past relationship patterns, and efficient, though not necessarily appropriate or effective.

Human communication behavior is so complex that Mom's response is typical—actually, a majority of communication behavior takes place mindlessly (Kellermann, 1992). For another example, think about simply replying to a friend's "How's it going?" while passing in the hall. To respond you must select and coordinate your words ("Good. Wassup?"), pitch, tone, inflection, facial expressions, and keep walking to the meeting you are late for. It is too much behavior to manage consciously. So mindlessness in predictable situations actually helps us out. However, while mindlessness may contribute to efficiency of response in many situations, conflict is a complex, unpredictable context that requires creative, mindful responses to the present, rather than overlearned responses to the past (Bavelas & Coates, 1992). As such, while it is beneficial to cultivate positive mindless responses for certain aspects of particular situations, we must also learn to mindfully adapt within our present circumstances—especially during conflict.

Managing Arousal to Stay in the Present

Arousal is a physiological state of activation that affects how we communicate. Here is how it works. Our bodies activate in response to external stimuli. Moderate to moderately high levels of activation are generally associated with good performance (like an athlete who gets "up" for a game). However, when we perceive a threat in our environment, our arousal levels may spike, reducing our ability to respond productively. This is a common occurrence during conflict. John Gottman (1994) describes how this process can create problems for married couples: "Increased diffuse physiological arousal makes it unlikely that the couple will be able to process information very well, will have access to new learning, and more likely that they will rely on previously overlearned tactics" (p. 412). In essence, when arousal is high, we are more likely to engage in mindlessness (overlearned tactics), which as we saw previously, reduces our ability to adapt to complex interactions with our partner in creative and constructive ways.

To make matters potentially worse, as long-term partners we may trigger negatively reciprocated patterns in one another, creating runaway conflict (Kelley, 2012). Runaway conflict is that experience where, in spite of positive goals for the interaction ("I'm going to stay calm, no matter what she says"), the conflict just seems to run out of control—my arousal spikes in response to something you say or do (that little snarky tone of voice), you sense my resistance and become defensive, I increase my defensiveness in response to your defensiveness, and so on and so forth. Before you know it, our plans for a productive discussion have turned into hurtful comments or withdrawal. As such, a critical element to creating engaging conflict is to keep partners' arousal levels in a moderate range. We will discuss practical ideas for managing arousal in the next section, however, before we make that move, I want to highlight how mindlessness and arousal work together to shift our attention from the problem at hand to relationship and identity goals.

Relationship Messages

Part of the reason our performance increases as arousal increases is that arousal serves as a focusing agent—you're "on," zeroed in. However, when arousal levels are too high it restricts our ability to attend to and process incoming information, and to develop creative responses. This state of "hyper-focus" can limit our ability to interpret incoming messages. Consider the following exchange:

Tom:	(*arriving home from work*) "I'm starving, is dinner ready?"
Kimberly:	(*just arrived home from picking up the kids*) "Definitely! I took off work early so that I could fix you dinner, pick up the children from day care, and then later tonight after they go to bed and I've finished the dishes, I'll finish the project I couldn't finish because I left work early!" (*stated with sarcasm*)
Tom:	What's up with you? I'll just get a beer with Damian. (*leaves abruptly*)

Let's unpack this scenario. Tom's seemingly innocent inquiry is heard by Kimberly as an attack—"I expect you to have dinner ready for me." Kimberly has felt that she pulls most of the weight when it comes to family "duties," along with trying to build her career, so Tom's comment spiked her arousal and sent her into hyper-focus. Earlier in their relationship when Kimberly felt things were more equally balanced, she may have generated a more creative, productive response to his inquiry, "Tom, I just got home with the kids. If you're hungry, why don't you pour some wine for the two of us, slice some cheese, and figure out what we can have for dinner?"

Hyper-focus tends to orient us to relationship and identity goals, triggering a focus on facework (see Chapter Eight: "Saving Face"). Although Kimberly's initial statement has content about dinner, the underlying relationship message is about equity and justice in the relationship. If Kimberly put words to her relationship issues it might sound like this: "I feel like you don't take my job seriously and expect me to do all the family chores, including care for the kids. It's just not fair!" Yet, like many of us, she has chosen instead to protect face and voice her feelings and concerns using sarcasm. Embedded in this conflict is one of the most common issues negotiated in relationships—power.

Power

Power is a commonly negotiated relationship issue. Furthermore, it is central to establishing social justice. Power exists in all relationships, and is present in all interactions. It can be used for ill or good, but in and of itself it is no more moral than gravity. However, common statements, such as, "That's not fair!" "Wait a minute, I was going to do that," "I'm not going to always say 'yes' to you anymore," and, as I once said to my mom, "I'll do it because I want to, not because you told me to," are all power-focused attempts at establishing dominance or equality. The key for us is to understand how to balance power to create interpersonal relationships.

Power is defined by McDonald (1980) as the capacity to attain one's goals. Thus, implicitly, power is the potential to influence others, and often results in dominance during interactions or the creation of dominant roles. As such, in order to keep power balanced in our relationships, we must recognize our power capabilities in a relationship and choose whether, or how, we might use this power.

According to McDonald, power can be exhibited in terms of bases, process, or outcomes. Bases refer to resources varying from economics (having money or having a good job) to personal characteristics (e.g., being good at math or being good looking) to cultural norms (e.g., being the oldest or being male). Processes are communication elements that, for our purposes, can include: one-up statements, verbal aggression, or assertiveness; conversation management elements such as interrupting, or dominating the amount of speaking time; and nonverbal displays such as fluent speech, loudness, body positioning, and gesturing. Outcomes demonstrate power by determining who actually achieves their goals. An example of the interplay of these three elements comes from a young, female, Pacific Rim student of mine, Malee. When Malee participated in small groups, in my class, she appeared to have few power bases (she was shy and didn't understand American culture very well) and few power processes (she seldom offered her opinion and when she did it was a struggle because English was difficult for her), however, in terms of outcomes, she always got her way. At least in the short-run, Malee's group members wanted to help her and felt awkward arguing with her, so often her opinion prevailed.

Handling the power dilemma involves creating spaces where power is equally shared. In the preceding example with Malee, if her group was to continue meeting for a long period of time and had more at stake, they would inevitably have to negotiate a better power balance between group members. Blau (1986) asserts that power is based on the extent to which we are dependent or independent on others and from this perspective offers four ways of balancing power. Following, I've modified his work for our purposes. First, to balance power, maintain alternative sources for what you need. This could include having multiple financial resources and good social support (friends and family). Second, develop resources that your partner needs. In other words, are you contributing to the relationship in a way that is valued by your partner? One manifestation of this is asset-based work with urban poor that focuses on the positive elements inherent in poor communities. As we discussed regarding advocacy (Chapter Five: "Interpersonal Advocacy"), the persons "helping" these communities and those who live there both benefit from their relationship. Third, when necessary, build coalitions. There is strength in numbers. Build important alliances with people who are valued in your social network. The intent of this is not to strong-arm your opponent, but to demonstrate the importance of the issue at hand, or to bolster your own credibility. Finally, be willing to do without. Again, this is not to manipulate your partner ("You can keep your ball, I'm going home!"), but instead to set appropriate boundaries (see Chapter Thirteen: "The Art of Reconciliation: Imagining a Just Future"). Being willing to do without involves telling your partner that you value them, but there are parameters as to how you can stay engaged in the relationship. For example, a partner who is having an affair and tells his partner that he is confused could be answered with, "I want to see if we can work this out, but I will only work on our relationship if you end the affair."

The foregoing suggestions for power balancing can also be used proactively to empower your partner by making certain she is not overly dependent on you. Help your partner find alternative sources of supply, build social support networks, and build important coalitions. According to mediation experts Bush and Folger (2005), empowerment also consists of strengthening one's self-worth and building confidence in one's own personal abilities. As such, some of the strategies we discussed in Chapter Eight: "Saving Face" could be used here to strengthen your own, or your partner's, self-worth: honoring, politeness, generosity, and support. In addition, we can empower ourselves and our partners by becoming competent in areas we care about.

Transcendent Discourse

Engaging conflict *transcends* traditional win-lose power structures and helps partners see themselves and their life situations in new ways. Pearce and Little-john (1997) suggest that moral conflict (conflict based on our deep values of right-wrong, good-bad) is best managed through transcendent conversations that "embody a series of turns that can allow us to discover new and positive resources for change" (p. 212). This sense of transcendence (the idea that we can think and act outside of what is normal or comfortable) is achieved by moving beyond overly simplistic responses to considering the "heart of the matter" (p. 213), moving beyond overly quick judgment to jointly explore similarities and differences, moving beyond creating obstructions to engaging genuine dialogue where we listen and value the other person, and moving beyond blame to collaborative problem-solving.

Engaging Conflict

Creating socially just relationships involves engaging conflict. Specifically, we must learn to manage arousal and mindless patterns of response, and find ways to balance power between conflicting parties. Most critical is using the principles we've been grappling with throughout this book to create transcendent interactions.

Putting Arousal and Mindlessness to Work

As we discussed previously, moderate levels of arousal work to our benefit, while high levels inhibit our ability to process information and respond creatively. The goal is to keep arousal at moderate levels so mindfulness and creativity are possible. Positive mindless patterns actually provide the freedom for mindfulness, by freeing our conscious minds from having to focus on routine, predictable activities. The key during conflict is managing arousal in order to prevent runaway conflict.

A beginning place to inhibit runaway conflict is to know one's own, and one's partner's, trigger points. What is it that sets off your partner and you, such that you feel somewhat out of control? (Like, when you are in a disagreement and tell yourself to just "let it go" and then hear yourself saying something you know you'll regret.) Next, practice active arousal reduction. Driver, Tabares, Shapiro, Nahm, and Gottman (2003) recommend conflicting partners take a 20-minute break, during conflict, to allow arousal levels to settle. This means allowing the mind to calm, and not ruminating. Other ways of moderating arousal include doing something physical, like taking a walk, running, swimming, or boxing; doing something communicative, like venting to a friend or counselor; changing one's environment, like going outside or to a favorite restaurant; and doing something spiritual, like praying or meditating, breathing deeply, or journaling. Long-term partners may actually plan ways to reduce arousal, together. For instance, make a habit of finishing your conversations while walking through the neighborhood, plan your budget on the patio of a local inexpensive restaurant, or have a difficult meeting in a neutral, pleasant environment.

> *Living It Out: What are your trigger points? What are your partner's? Since trigger points are predictable, how can you plan ahead to avoid spikes in arousal when trigger points occur?*
>
> *Living It Out: What are your best arousal reduction techniques? With your partner, talk about the best ways to keep arousal in the moderate range during your conflicts. Make a plan as to how to work as a team to keep arousal under control (e.g., like being willing to take a 20-minute break when needed).*

Power Balancing

As conflicts heat up, they often shift from content to relationship issues. At the core of many relationship issues is power. Power is most often dealt with indirectly, by talking about who takes out the trash, who works hardest, or what kind of car you're going to buy. However, when culturally appropriate, we can learn to put our perceived inequities on the table. That is, in a way that respects our partner, we can offer our perspective about how the relationship could be more equal for both of us. In addition, we can make choices that empower our partners. We can open ourselves up and be vulnerable, and value what they bring to the relationship. We can allow them to grow and change and be less dependent on us. And, we can encourage them to build strong social support and continue to develop their skill sets, and honor them, be polite and generous, and supportive.

> *Living It Out: Think of power bases, processes, and outcomes in your relationship. When taken as a whole, is there a balance of power in your relationship? How would your relationship partner answer that question?*
>
> *Living It Out: How can you empower your relationship partner? How can you empower yourself? Make a private list of things you can do and work on one way to empower yourself or your partner each week this month.*

Transcendent Living

Transcendent living is living in a way that is resilient and forward thinking. It is characterized by openness and creativity, and the ability and willingness to adapt to a changing environment. To live transcendentally is to 1) reflect deeply on your experience considering the "heart of the matter"; 2) openly, nondefensively, and honestly explore similarities and differences with your partner; 3) resist obstructing your partner's thinking and decisions and, rather, trust the wisdom and influence of genuine dialogue between genuine partners; and 4) resist blaming, instead trusting your partner enough that you can critically examine issues and creatively problem solve together.

Living It Out: Identify the parts of transcendent living at which you are particularly adept. How about your partner?

Living It Out: Select one of the four characteristics of transcendent living to further develop this week. Knowing your conflict triggers, how will you be proactive in living transcendentally (list specific behaviors or changes in thinking)?

Case 11.1

Courtney and Belinda have been sisters for 45 years—Courtney is the oldest, 51, and Belinda, the "baby" sister. Last week, their mom passed away from breast cancer. Dad passed two years previous. Planning the memorial service and taking care of the estate has created more than one conflict between the sisters. Courtney, as the oldest, is now trustee of the estate, and has taken the reins in terms of planning the memorial service. However, Mom had specifically talked with Belinda about her impending service, because Belinda is the more creative and sensitive of the two.

Although Courtney and Belinda have always loved each other, like many sister relationships they've had their share of fighting. With the added stress of grieving the loss of their mom, conflicts erupt quickly. One of their conflicts went something like this:

Courtney: Okay, so we're going to need someone to sing at the service.

Belinda: Mom told me she didn't want music, she just wanted someone to read Scripture.

Courtney: She never told me that.

Belinda: Well . . .

Courtney: Well, what?

Belinda: Maybe she tried, but gave up because you don't listen. She told me lots of things.

Courtney: Look, Mom told everyone lots of things . . . during her last days she was drugged up half the time and didn't know what she was saying. We still need someone to sing.

Belinda: You can't stand the fact that Mom could talk to me. Just 'cuz you're oldest doesn't mean you run the show. I have a voice here.

Courtney: Yes, you have a voice, but I do run the show. I have power of attorney and am trustee, so where does that leave you?

Belinda: Fine, run your little show by yourself! See you at the service. (*picks up her purse and leaves the house*)

Processing

1. Courtney and Belinda have had 45 years to develop patterns of managing conflict. In what ways is their relationship system resisting change?

2. How are mindlessness and arousal affecting this interaction? What do you think are Courtney and Belinda's conflict triggers?

3. How is power a factor in this interaction? Suggest some possible ways to balance power between them.

4. Discuss elements of this conflict that are transcendent, or not transcendent.

Case 11.2

Sam is 21, outgoing, and an average student at school. He comes from a single-parent family that has few financial resources, but where everyone played sports in hopes of one day, as his dad would say, "buying a ticket out of town." In this light, another of his dad's mottos is: "Quitting isn't an option!" Once you start a sport, you finish out the season. As Sam has gotten older, staying on a team has been tough, but he is currently one of four relief pitchers for the small college he attends in Eastern Washington. Five weeks into the season Sam is tired of playing baseball, and his grades are suffering. He is frustrated and has thought a few times about quitting the team and trying to get his grades up so he can eventually apply for graduate school. But, his dad doesn't understand the idea of graduate school and sees sports as his only way of eventually having a career.

Sam tried to raise the issue with his dad, how dropping the team would mean he could focus on school, but his dad looked upset and diverted the discussion using another of his favorite phrases: "Hard work is ever rewarded." In his dad's mind, he is encouraging Sam. In Sam's mind, his dad is pushing him to do what he (dad) wants him to do. Even though Sam is a leader of a large campus club and involved in student government debates, when he talks with his dad it's like he is a 10-year-old kid again. No matter what goals he goes in with, once his dad starts talking, Sam feels his anxiety increase and then just falls into old patterns of doing what his dad wants.

One day, talking to his girlfriend, Abby, about the situation, she finally told him, "You need to be your own person. Your dad owns you." Sam actually likes these "hard" discussions with Abby. They are unlike anything he ever experienced at home. Even though their discussions are often challenging, they talk deeply about things and can be really honest with each other. Abby seldom blames him for things or puts a lot of guilt on him. Instead, her style is to tell him straight up, "Here's how I see things. We need to talk about this," and then, somehow he feels empowered to give his opinion, too.

Regarding the team, Sam thinks about Abby's comments and finally decides he needs to have a real talk with his dad.

Processing

1. How is Sam's relationship with his dad resisting change?

2. How is mindlessness and arousal affecting this interaction for Sam and his dad?

3. How might the power imbalance between Sam and his dad be affecting Sam's inability to do what he wants?

4. Discuss how the conversations/conflicts Sam has with Abby exhibit the principles of transcendent living.

References

Allende, I. (2014). How to live passionately—no matter your age. https://www.ted.com/talks/isabelle_allende_how_to_live_passionately_no_matter_your_age?language=en

Bavelas, J. B., & Coates, L. (1992). How do we account for the mindfulness of face-face dialogue? *Communication Monographs, 59*, 301–305.

Blau, P. M. (1986). *Exchange and power in social life.* New Brunswick: Transaction Books.

Burpee, L. C., & Langer, E. J. (2005). Mindfulness and marital satisfaction. *Journal of Adult Development, 12*, 43–51.

Bush, R. A. B., & Folger, J. P. (2005). *The promise of mediation: The transformative approach to conflict.* San Francisco: Jossey-Bass.

Driver, J., Tabares, A., Shapiro, A., Nahm, E. Y., & Gottman, J. M. (2003). Interactional patterns in marital success and failure: Gottman laboratory. In F. Walsh (Ed.), *Normal family processes: Growing diversity and complexity* (3rd ed., pp. 493–513). New York: Guilford Press.

Galvin, C. M., Dickson, F. C., & Marrow, S. R. (2006). Systems theory: Patterns and (w)holes in family communication. In D. O. Braithwaite & L. A. Baxter (Eds.), *Engaging theories in family communication: Multiple perspectives* (pp. 309–324). Thousand Oaks, CA: Sage.

Gottman, J. M. (1994). *What predicts divorce? The relationship between marital processes and marital outcomes.* Hillsdale, NJ: Erlbaum.

Kellermann, K. (1992). Communication: Inherently strategic and primarily automatic. *Communication Monographs, 59*, 288–300.

Kelley, D. L. (2012). *Marital communication.* Cambridge, UK: Polity.

Langer, E. J. (1989). *Mindfulness.* Reading, MA: Addison-Wesley.

McDonald, G. W. (1980). Family power: The assessment of a decade of theory and research, 1970–1979. *Journal of Marriage and Family, 42*(4), 841–854.

Pearce, W. B., & Littlejohn, S. W. (1997). *Moral conflict: When social worlds collide.* Thousand Oaks, CA: Sage.

Tutu, D. M. (1999). *No future without forgiveness.* New York: Random House.

Watzlawick, P., Beavin, J. H., & Jackson, D. D. (1967). *Pragmatics of human communication.* New York: Norton.

12

FORGIVENESS

Choosing How You Want to Live

"There is no way I am letting him off the hook for what he's done." "I am not going to just excuse the way she treated me." "After what he put me through, I hope, someday, somebody does the same to him." "Just wait. She'll get what she deserves!" The foregoing statements sound familiar to most of us, and exemplify why many of us are resistant to forgive. Yet, they also represent misunderstandings about the nature of forgiveness.

In some ways, talking about forgiveness seems to be exactly opposite of talking about *just relationships*. In fact, the preceding nonforgiveness statements all represent a desire for justice. They recognize the inherent problems in "letting someone off the hook" or excusing hurtful behavior. Justice, when discussing relationship hurt and transgression, is often associated with balancing (equity) the pain experienced in a hurtful situation, and victims and offenders both "getting what they deserve" (see Chapter Two: "Just Relationships").

So why talk about forgiveness here? Two reasons. First, forgiveness is an extension of resilience. It is one of the ways we become resilient people and create resilient relationships. Without forgiveness we stay locked in our pain and bitterness, and are inhibited from creating fully just futures for ourselves, and the partners for whom we care. Second, through forgiveness, we heal the past, and move forward toward a just future. Without forgiveness we stay locked into models of justice based on the complete monitoring of one another's behaviors. As we discussed in the first four chapters of the book, sustainable interpersonal justice is dependent on a change of the heart, a movement toward dialogue wherein we co-create spaces where *if something good can happen, it will.*

I begin this chapter by looking at the nature of hurt. I then position forgiveness as one means of healing interpersonal pain. Choosing this course of action involves five essential elements of the forgiveness process (Kelley, 1998; Waldron & Kelley, 2008). The second half of the chapter, *Freedom through Forgiveness*, profiles two approaches that help us practically do forgiveness.

Reeling from Our Pain

Those who believe they are living in unjust, unfair conditions endure significant relational pain. A number of researchers have been seeking to understand the nature of relationship hurt and pain. They have found that relationship hurt is largely a function of an emotional response to personal injury, typically from some type of perceived relationship transgression or other personal devaluation from one's partner (Kelley, 2012b).

Feeney (2005, 2009) uses attachment theory to understand personal injury. In Chapter Six: "Worldview," we discussed attachment theory as a way that individuals create relationship frames with which to view the world. Feeney believes that when these attachment models (relationship frames) are disturbed (through hurtful behaviors, such as disassociation, criticism, and betrayal) the hurt relationship partner reassesses her own self and her partner. Specifically, she reassesses her own loveworthiness (e.g., "How do I keep ending up in abusive relationships? Is there something wrong with me?"), and her partner's availability, responsiveness, and trustworthiness (e.g., "Is my partner who I thought she was?" "Can I ever be vulnerable with her, or will she not respond well when I express how I feel?").

Vangelisti (2009) reminds us that episodes in which we are hurt by others are complex events. They are often combinations of specific actions (e.g., sexual infidelity is often accompanied by deception). This facilitates complex emotional responses to the hurt. Someone who has been blindsided by his partner's betrayal may feel shock, sadness, anger, and even eventually be surprised by positive emotions such as love or compassion.

Forgiveness: Freedom from the Constraints of Negative Emotion

Harboring negative emotion for extended periods of time is not healthy for us physically, psychologically, or relationally. One way to manage our negative emotion is to engage the forgiveness process (Toussaint, Owen, & Cheadle, 2011; Webb, Hirsch, Visser, & Brewer, 2013). Forgiveness is *not* stuffing your emotions, or avoiding conflict, or tolerating bad behavior. Forgiveness is not excusing your partner's irresponsibility in order to protect his feelings so that you don't have to deal with your pain. Instead, forgiveness is a process that restores our emotional, physical, and relational health (Kelley, Wolf, & Broberg, 2016).

Forgiveness has been studied from numerous perspectives. Before proceeding, take a moment to write your own definition of forgiveness. Next, write out the relational implications of your definition—that is, in what ways does forgiveness affect how you maintain, repair, or decide to stay in your relationships? This is basically what Vince Waldron and I have done over the past two decades. We developed the following forgiveness definition in order to emphasize the social aspects of forgiveness, and the creation of socially *just relationships*:

> Forgiveness is a relational process whereby harmful conduct is acknowledged by one or both partners; the harmed partner extends undeserved mercy to

the perceived transgressor; one or both partners experience a transformation from negative to positive psychological states, and the meaning of the relationship is renegotiated, with the possibility of reconciliation.

(Waldron & Kelley, 2008, p. 19)

Hard and Soft Emotions

As we consider the role of forgiveness in emotional healing, it is important to recognize that "negative" emotions aren't all the same. Sanford (2007) distinguishes between hard emotions, such as anger, power, and control, and soft emotions, such as sadness and hurt. Hard emotions reflect more self-focused goals and are associated with blaming, competition, and self-preservation behaviors. Soft emotions are more prosocial and associated with vulnerability. As we do forgiveness, we seek to diminish our hard negative emotions over a reasonable time, while soft emotions may linger, in healthy ways, for years. For example, regarding your brother's suicide, leaving behind a wife and three young children, over time you may let go of your initial anger (this seemed such a selfish act), but you will likely always have a pang of deep sadness over the loss of your brother.

Voicing Our Thoughts and Emotions

One way of letting go of one's hard emotions is by giving voice to them and the thoughts that accompany them. Voicing one's emotions and thoughts can take various forms including telling the offender how you feel, venting to a friend or counselor, or expressing oneself through other means such as journaling (Waldron & Kelley, 2008). Giving voice to one's experience can also take the form of verbalized prayer, which can help manage emotion and sort through one's thinking as the relational crisis is processed (Beach, Fincham, Hurt, McNair, & Stanley, 2008; Kelley, 2012c). Voicing one's feelings and thinking, whether to a safe partner, oneself (journaling), or God, can provide a means of making sense of what has happened and what is yet to come, while potentially reducing high arousal levels.

Developing Empathy

The process of giving voice to feelings and thoughts, and subsequent reduced arousal levels, gives possibility to empathizing with the person who hurt you. Empathy is an essential sense-making and emotional-response element of the forgiveness process (Malcolm, Warwar, & Greenberg, 2005; McCullough, Worthington, & Rachal, 1997; Waldron & Kelley, 2008). Empathizing with the offender rehumanizes her through more fully understanding her situation. It is important to realize that empathizing *does not excuse* the offender from her hurtful behavior. However, it can help you feel compassion for the offender as a broken person. Suppose your father was abusive to you as a child. As an adult you are angry about this, but then you find out your father was abused, as a child, by his father. This new information helps you *empathize* with your father's experience, *but not excuse it.* You can feel compassion for him, but recognize that he had choices as an adult to act differently. As such, empathy allows us to shift our emotions from negative to positive (e.g., from anger to compassion), rehumanizing the other person as we see them in their own context, and, yet, still holding them accountable for their actions.

Forward through Forgiveness

In 2011, I was in Amman, Jordan and the West Bank speaking about interpersonal forgiveness. A Palestinian who had been listening to my presentation came up to me at a break and asked, "How can we ever forgive Israel for what they have done to us?" Obviously it was an important question, heavy on his heart. I had two minutes to respond before returning to the platform. I am not a political scholar, but I do understand the potential power of forgiveness. I looked him in the eyes and replied, "I can't tell you that you should forgive. But the question for you is, how do you want to live? How do you want your children to live?"

Frequently people hesitate to forgive because forgiveness seems unfair. When not properly understood, it seems to give little heed to the person's deep pain, and even fails to take into account the entrenched loyalty one often feels to family and friends who have been hurt. According to Desmond Tutu in *No Future Without Forgiveness*, this was the dilemma of South Africans when they created truth and reconciliation commissions. They had to decide how to move forward, honoring those who had been killed or injured in the political struggle, acknowledging the deep pain of their families, yet, creating a country of new possibilities with their perpetrators.

Forgiveness was the answer. As we've discussed, forgiveness requires truth be acknowledged regarding wrongs done. But truth also recognizes that there is no perfect justice for these very wrongs. What can ever make things "equal" for the loss of a child, spouse, or close friend? Or the loss of one's home? There is no perfect justice for these things. However, when we forgive we seek justice in the sense that we do not excuse or tolerate or avoid. Forgiveness *always* recognizes that a wrong has been done. Yet, forgiveness also *always* rehumanizes the offender, *creating space where if something good can happen, it will.*

Following, I offer two ways to think through the forgiveness process. And, process it is. Forgiveness can take weeks, years, or a lifetime. But, it is a worthy journey toward a just future, freed from our anger, bitterness, and hate.

A Relational Process

There are five essential elements to this definition. First, as I've noted, we focus on the experience of forgiveness as a relational process. Historically forgiveness has primarily been understood as a practice that occurs between God and humankind or between people, instead of purely as a psychological process. In this vein, I have been interested in how forgiveness potentially restores persons and relationships after interpersonal injury and transgression have been experienced (Kelley, 2012a).

Recognizing Something Wrong Happened

A second aspect of this definition is recognizing harmful conduct. Generally, when we discuss forgiveness, harmful conduct is construed in moral terms—that is, I experience what happened to me as something that "shouldn't" have happened or, more pointedly, was "wrong"! Interestingly, for many, the forgiveness process stops at this early juncture. Pulitzer Prize nominated author Frederick Buechner (1993) has this to say about putting words to the events and people in our lives, "Something that lay hidden in the heart is irrevocably released through speech" (p. 121). He goes on to propose, "In a sense I do not love you first and then speak it, but only by speaking it give it reality" (p. 121). His extraordinary insight into the power of words, labeling and naming our experience, helps us understand why people are sometimes resistant to recognizing something "wrong" happened. For example, if at some point you decide to describe your parents as "abusive," you have changed the nature of your reality—and likely a personal and, possibly, interpersonal response is required. This is why many people forgive by trying to "return to normal" (a resilience strategy we discussed in Chapter Nine). It is a means of moving on without having to deal with harmful, unjust behavior. Therefore, the process of admitting that something "wrong" happened is a significant one as it pushes us to deal with our painful pasts.

Granting Undeserved Mercy

A third definitional aspect, extending undeserved mercy to the person who hurt you, is fundamental to most understandings of forgiveness. By *undeserved* we do not mean that people who hurt you are not worth your love and grace. *Undeserved* refers to the justice ethic we discussed in Chapter Two: "Just Relationships," and is reflected in the quotes at the beginning of this chapter. The justice motive we develop as children is the foundational belief that "people should get what they deserve" (Lerner, 2002). In that sense, when we respond to others and forgo making certain that they fully get what they deserve, we are granting undeserved mercy.

Our research demonstrates that people grant this undeserved mercy in a number of ways (Waldron & Kelley, 2005, 2008). Of course, one strategy is to explicitly state, "I forgive you," although this is mostly used for severe transgressions. Other strategies are less direct. Discussing the event to create understanding and showing sincerity of emotion nonverbally (e.g., crying, hugging) are two ways that people forgive without necessarily saying "forgive." These means of granting forgiveness can be especially effective when combined with direct statements of forgiveness. Also, as already mentioned, many people simply try to act "normal" again or minimize the offense, "Hey, no big deal." Often these approaches mean partners never talk about the hurtful issue, they just attempt to return to how they have typically behaved with one another. These have certain short-term benefits, like protecting the offender's face and avoiding direct confrontation, however partners miss out on the long-term benefits of understanding and emotional healing. A final tactic, conditional forgiveness ("I'll forgive you if . . ."), is frequently used in conjunction with severe transgressions. However, conditional forgiveness can have mixed effects on the relationship. Unilaterally placing conditions on one's relational partner may be interpreted as a power move or manipulation and, as such, undermine the sense of equality and respect in the relationship. (In contrast to granting forgiveness conditionally, in Chapter Thirteen: "The Art of Reconciliation: Imagining a Just Future," I discuss the process of setting appropriate boundaries in relationships.)

Transformation from Negative to Positive

A fourth element of forgiveness involves a shift from negative to positive psychological states, and often a subsequent shift toward positive feelings and behavior toward the offending partner. This involves two forgiveness processes, making sense of what has happened and managing one's emotions. Once a relationship transgression has been detected individuals experience an immediate emotional response and subsequent cognitive processing to determine what this means. The two of these processes are often deeply intertwined. For example, if I found out you told our friends something that I had told you in confidence, I would likely feel betrayed, angry, and hurt. These emotions would trigger thinking about myself and you, as we discussed previously under the section on hurt—"What is wrong with me?" "Can I trust you?" Subsequently, these assessments may trigger other emotions, such as depression or hopelessness, which may trigger new thinking (that often becomes more and more extreme, "I'll *never* find a trustworthy partner!"), *ad infinitum*. In actuality, the interplay between our emotional response and how we think is often experienced as a seamless interchange.

Renegotiating the Relationship

Finally, interpersonal forgiveness involves renegotiating the relationship, with the possibility of reconciliation. It is extremely important to recognize that *forgiveness is not the same as reconciliation*. Many people reject forgiveness because they think forgiving requires them to reconcile with their offender. You can forgive without reconciling, and you can reconcile without forgiveness (though the reconciliation will likely not be a full reconciliation). Full forgiveness opens the doors for reconciliation when conditions are safe and the relationship is still desired. I talk more fully about reconciliation in the next chapter (Chapter Thirteen: "The Art of Reconciliation: Imagining a Just Future," but for our purposes here we must realize that, often, interpersonal forgiveness talk is entangled with clarifying relationship guidelines and negotiating a new moral order for the relationship. A necessary reminder, however, is that this relationship talk may result in one or both parties deciding they are no longer interested in continuing the relationship. In this case, either unilaterally or together, the relationship may be terminated.

TUF Forgiveness

TUF is an acronym reminding us that forgiveness takes great courage. TUF represents forgiveness as truth, understanding, and freedom. The *truth* of the matter is that we believe that something "wrong" or "bad" has happened to us. But there are also other truths we must grasp. The truth is, I have failed and hurt others, as well. It is the human condition. We are not perfect. Therefore, the offender's "bad" behavior doesn't make him a bad person. And, the true nature of significant relationships is that we are interdependent on one another, and therefore vulnerable, and prone to be disappointed and hurt at times. However, this is all balanced with a final truth—we *can* survive what we are currently going through, we *can* heal our pain, and we *can* create a better life for ourselves and others.

Understanding represents self- and other-discovery. First, as I have emphasized throughout the book, I seek to understand myself. How does what has happened to me help me better know who I am? What does my emotional response say about me, and the way I live, and what I expect? Second, having had the courage to look at my own self, I seek to understand the one who offended me and, through this process, allow them to become human to me again. Understanding puts things in context—I now see the person who hurt me in light of his imperfect past. And, I have the opportunity to feel empathy and compassion for my perpetrator's own painful life, without excusing his own poor choices. (Note that understanding self and other don't necessarily occur in any particular order. Most often these are parallel processes that take time.)

Finally, we choose to be *free* from our hard negative emotions (anger, bitterness, rage) by extending the gift of forgiveness. As one of the respondents in our study stated, "You think you are giving the other person a gift, but then you realize forgiveness is for yourself" (Waldron & Kelley, 2008). Give voice to your forgiveness, but, remember, only tell the person you are forgiving them if they are safe for you to be with physically and emotionally. Other good options are to tell a friend or a counselor or write it in your journal. Remember, when you put words to it, it becomes more real.

> *Living It Out: Are you harboring pain that you need to acknowledge? The truth of forgiveness could be the answer, but only start down this path if you have a safe environment to do so—remember, putting words to your pain can make it seem more real. Take a minute to evaluate your support system—do you have at least one good friend, a mentor, or counselor to support you in this process?*
>
> *Living It Out: Consider the person who hurt you. What is their current life situation? Are they under stress? Do they have the personal skills to handle conflict well? Are they grappling with their own pain? What about their past? Have past experiences crippled them from living as a complete, loving human being? Considering these things, can you rehumanize this person? Can you see them as a hurting, broken human being, instead of only seeing them as a heartless offender?*
>
> *Living It Out: Be really honest with this question—Do you want freedom from your pain and anger? Some of us are so used to feeling negative emotions that we don't*

want to be free from them. Once you decide you want to let go of your hard emotions, decide to make the gift of forgiveness—for yourself and, maybe, for the other person. Only tell the person who hurt you if they are safe for you physically and emotionally. Be sure to tell someone else (even your journal) that you have chosen freedom!

Offering the Hand of Forgiveness

I want to finish this section by offering one other way to think through the forgiveness process—the *Hand of Forgiveness*. This concrete analogy really works for me, but it is also great with children. Raise your left hand and look at it, palm side up. The thumb reminds us that something happened to us, something hurtful. With children, and when I'm feeling particularly brave, I tell them to remember this as "*Thumb*thing happened to me."

The index finger is our pointer finger. Pointing at someone can represent blame. In this case, the pointer finger represents trying to make sense out of what happened. To picture this, point to your temple as though you just had a new idea. This part of the process focuses on you and your offender, and is characterized by the questions we asked earlier: "Am I loveworthy?" "Will you be available to me?" "Will you be responsive to me?" "Can I trust you?" Of course, people often also consider, "Why did this happen to me?" "Are you who I thought you were?" "What does this potentially change about our relationship?"

The middle finger is our emotional response. For appropriately aged audiences, I remind them that this finger, when placed in a particular position, is often used to tell people how we feel. Another way to think about this is the middle finger is often the finger that gets injured because it sticks out farther than the others. After using this finger to think through your emotional response, intertwine the index and middle fingers as a reminder that there is great strength when you process your emotions and your thinking together—this represents the full sense of what has happened to you.

The ring finger represents commitment. Rings often represent commitment to persons, ideals, or institutions. Regarding *just relationships*, this first of all represents my commitment to live a healthy life, free from unhealthy patterns of living. Second is my commitment to healthy relationships—*just relationships* that are characterized by equality and respect. Third, my commitment is to treating you in a compassionate and just manner. I am committed to creating a space where you are free to grow. Wearing a ring can be a great way to signify this full commitment to another person or to a way of life.

Finally, the pinky finger represents giving forgiveness. It is seemingly the weakest of all the fingers, but it balances the hand. It gives us a full grip. Remember "pinky swears"—interlocking your pinkies and shaking on an agreement—with friends in grade school? Why the pinky? It represents our vulnerability with one another—yet, in light of this vulnerability, trust and interdependence. This is what *Part I* of this book was about—socially just relationships only result from love and advocacy—creating safe places *where if something good can happen, it will.*

> *Living It Out: Think of a person you would like to forgive. Holding your hand up, walk through the Hand of Forgiveness. When you hit a finger (forgiveness concept) that you are struggling with, be willing to stay in that place for awhile (e.g., it could take you weeks or months to process your emotions). Mark the finger where you are working—for instance, tie a string around your index finger because you are trying to make sense of what happened to you (or, if you're brave, paint your fingernail as a reminder!).*
>
> *Living It Out: If the person who hurt you is safe for you (emotionally and physically), share your forgiveness hand with them. Or, find a safe friend, mentor, or counselor with whom to share your forgiveness hand. Remember, putting words to your forgiveness will make it more real.*

Case 12.1

Carlos and Lidia have been together 15 years. They have three children, own a home in a good school district, are involved in local community organizations, and both hold down good jobs that require 50–60 hours a week. They care deeply for one another and are very happy with their family situation, but only get small amounts of time together as a couple because they are both so busy.

In the fall, Carlos's mother was diagnosed with an aggressive form of breast cancer that had begun to metastasize into her back and lungs. She passed away the following July. During this stressful time, Lidia began to find emotional support at work. Nothing was really "wrong" at home, but at work, one colleague, Devon, was particularly attentive to her. She felt guilty about it, but Devon's attention felt good since Carlos was typically preoccupied with managing his mom's passing, work, and the kids. Working late one evening, she was particularly sad and as Devon comforted her they kissed. She was startled at the strong feelings she had developed for him, yet she didn't want to destroy her family. So, the next day she apologized to Devon for letting things happen, and that night told Carlos about the incident.

Carlos felt blindsided when he heard what had happened. He was angry and threw a pillow across the room, breaking a vase that was above the fireplace. "How could you do this to me? Especially when my mom just died! I thought we were working really well together. I thought I knew who you are." Lidia just cried and said she was sorry. That night, and the next several, they slept in separate rooms. During this time Carlos got various advice from several buddies, but finally went on a 25-mile bike ride to think, and pray, and try to sort out what was happening to him. During this time he realized he still loved Lidia, but was confused and deeply hurt. On his return home, he got a babysitter and Lidia and he went out to dinner.

Conversation was awkward, at first. Then Lidia said, "I have nothing to lose, so I'm going to tell you what happened. I hadn't really paid attention to us drifting apart. Like you said, life was basically good. But when your mom died . . . well, I realized how far apart we were emotionally, and I guess it left me vulnerable. I told you what happened because I love you and still want to work on things. And, I know it's not enough to say it, but I'm *so* sorry." Her eyes were wet with tears and she was shaking. Carlos came to her side of the table and held her. "I don't know what's going to happen. I'm so hurt, but I also know that we were drifting apart, and I haven't always been the best at affirming you. It's just you always seem to be holding together so well."

"So," ventured Lidia, "are we going to try to work this out?"

There was a longer pause than Lidia was comfortable with, but finally Carlos said, "My family raised me—'eye for an eye.' When someone hurts us, we save face by hurting them back. But I don't want to hurt you. I want to see if we can somehow fix things."

"So are you saying you forgive me?" Lidia asked.

"I don't know," said Carlos. "I'm just saying I'm willing to see what happens."

Processing

1. Although it may seem obvious at first, use material from the chapter to describe what is at the core of Carlos's pain. How might Carlos and Lidia each begin to work through their own pain?

2. How is Carlos beginning to work through the TUF Forgiveness process? Using the TUF model, describe things he can do to work toward forgiveness?

3. Imagine being a good friend of Carlos. You know he and Lidia are great together. How would you use the *hand of forgiveness* to encourage Carlos to think about forgiving?

Case 12.2

Stacie's mom, Rae, had worked hard all of her life to have a career equal to that of her husband. She loved her kids, but wasn't really much of a "kid person." Instead, she loved the business world, travel, and politics. Both her and her husband's ambition, insecurities, and pride eventually led to a divorce after 22 years of marriage. Stacie and Tyson were born late into the marriage, and Stacie always resented the fact that, after the divorce, Ty, got to live with his dad (the "fun" parent), while she had to live with Mom.

When Stacie was 42, and Ty was 45, Rae entered into the early stages of Alzheimer's Disease. Ty lived out of state and traveled for his job and Stacie lived alone, so care for Mom was predetermined—she would move in with Stacie until her disease progressed enough that she needed constant care. Stacie resented, once again, having to live with and care for Mom.

One day after complaining to a friend about her situation, the friend gave her a couple quotes from author Anne Lamott. In talking about her mom, Lamott

(1999) writes that, "she is not at all whom I would have picked at the Neiman-Marcus Mommy Salon" (p. 209) and then later offers the following truth, "forgiveness is giving up all hope of having had a different past" (p. 213). It had never occurred to Stacie that she could forgive her mother for not being the person she (Stacie) wanted her to be. This started Stacie on a journey exploring her mom's past. She began by reading her mom's journals. Later, she emailed and made phone calls to her aunts and uncles, often asking questions about old family pictures and events. Through this process, Stacie began to experience freedom from much of the emotional pain in her past and, eventually, truly forgive her mom and care for her without resentment. She never directly told her mother about the forgiveness, but one night she called Ty and told him how she had decided she was "really okay taking care of Mom."

Processing

1. How did Stacie work through the TUF Forgiveness process? In particular, how did truth and understanding seem to free Stacie? Explain why (or why not) you think her forgiveness will continue over time.
2. How is Stacie offering the hand of forgiveness to her mother? Describe each finger and thumb and how they might apply to Stacie's forgiveness of her mother. In particular, how did Stacie use the index and middle fingers to begin her own healing?

References

Beach, S. R. H., Fincham, F. D., Hurt, T. R., McNair, L. M., & Stanley, S. M. (2008). Prayer and marital intervention: A conceptual framework. *Journal of Social and Clinical Psychology, 27*, 641–669.

Buechner, F. (1993). *Wishful thinking: A seeker's abc*. New York: Harper Collins.

Feeney, J. A. (2005). Hurt feelings in couple relationships: Exploring the role of attachment and perceptions of personal injury. *Personal Relationships, 12*, 255–271.

Feeney, J. A. (2009). When love hurts: Understanding hurtful events in couple relationships. In A. Vangelisti (Ed.), *Feeling hurt in close relationships* (pp. 313–335). New York: Cambridge University Press.

Kelley, D. L. (1998). The communication of forgiveness. *Communication Studies, 49*, 255–271.

Kelley, D. L. (2012a). Forgiveness as restoration: The search for well-being, reconciliation, and relational justice. In T. J. Socha & M. J. Pitts (Eds.), *The positive side of interpersonal communication* (pp. 193–209). New York: Peter Lang.

Kelley, D. L. (2012b). *Marital communication*. Cambridge, UK: Polity.

Kelley, D. L. (2012c). Prayer and forgiveness: Communication and Christian applications. *The Journal of Communication and Religion, 35*, 254–271.

Kelley, D. L., Wolf, B. M., & Broberg, S. E. (2016). Forgiveness, communication, and health. *The Oxford research encyclopedia of communication*. New York: Oxford University Press. doi: 10.1093/acrefore/9780190228613.013.9

Lamott, A. (1999). *Traveling mercies*. New York: Anchor Books.

Lerner, M. J. (2002). Pursuing the justice motive. In M. Ross & D. T. Miller (Eds.), *The justice motive in everyday life* (pp. 10–40). Cambridge: Cambridge University Press.

Malcolm, W., Warwar, S., & Greenberg, L. (2005). Facilitating forgiveness in individual therapy as an approach to resolving interpersonal injuries. In E. L. Worthington, Jr. (Ed.), *Handbook of forgiveness* (pp. 379–391). New York: Routledge.

McCullough, M. E., Worthington, E. L. Jr., & Rachal, K. C. (1997). Interpersonal forgiving in close relationships. *Journal of Personality and Social Psychology, 73*, 321–336.

Sanford, K. (2007). The couples emotion rating form: Psychometric properties and theoretical associations. *Journal of Social and Personal Relationships, 20*, 391–402.

Toussaint, L. L., Owen, A. D., & Cheadle, A. (2011). Forgive to live: Forgiveness, health, and longevity. *Journal of Behavioral Medicine, 35*, 375–386.

Tutu, D. M. (1999). *No future without forgiveness.* New York: Random House.

Vangelisti, A. L. (2009). Hurt feelings: Distinguishing features, functions, and overview. In A. L. Vangelisti (Ed.), *Feeling hurt in close relationships* (pp. 3–11). New York: Cambridge University Press.

Waldron, V. R., & Kelley, D. L. (2005). Forgiveness as a response to relational transgression. *Journal of Personality and Social Psychology, 22*, 723–742.

Waldron, V. R., & Kelley, D. L. (2008). *Communicating forgiveness.* Thousand Oaks, CA: Sage.

Webb, J. R., Hirsch, J. K., Visser, P. L., & Brewer, K. G. (2013). Forgiveness and health: Assessing the mediating effect of health behavior, social support, and interpersonal functioning. *The Journal of Psychology, 147*(5), 391–414.

13

THE ART OF RECONCILIATION

Imagining a Just Future

Reconciliation takes many forms. One of the respondents in my first forgiveness study told me that she hadn't spoken to a close friend for almost two years. Then, one day she realized that she was no longer angry and, out of the blue, contacted her. They ended up getting together, found they were back on equal footing, and rekindled their friendship. Quickly, they felt like they were best friends again.

A cohabiting couple in a later study told me the story of how they had been married, then divorced, and now were living together. He wanted to remarry, but she liked her new experience of equality and didn't want to do anything to jeopardize it at this point (she joked that he was still writing her a monthly alimony check for $1000!).

A friend who grew up in an abusive family system left home at 16 with the intention of never coming back. For three years . . . no contact. However, through social media her brother finally tracked her down, and they began hanging out every month or so. He finally told his parents that he was seeing his sister on a regular basis and asked if he could invite her to Thanksgiving. They were nervous, but said, "yes." For the last four years she has been coming home, three to four times a year for family events.

Each of these events represents a form or degree of reconciliation. The first example is full reconciliation—both friends are past their emotional pain and are re-committed to each other with a new sense of trust in the relationship. The cohabiting partners are living in the same space again and have a certain level of commitment to each other. However, the wife's pain is still lingering along with a lack of trust as to what the future may hold. The runaway daughter, from the abusive family system, is back because she cares for her brother, but the pain from her childhood is still with her. She wants to trust that things have changed at home, but she is extremely hesitant to commit herself to the family as a whole.

When conditions are right, the chapters of this book lead to the end goal of reconciliation. Yet, it is clear that full reconciliation is not always appropriate, as *not all relationships or relationship partners are safe*. It is important to realize when to get out of unhealthy relationships. However, the focus of this volume has been how to transform our existing relationships, or grow our new relationships, into *just relationships*. Thus, this final chapter begins by looking at three foundational aspects of reconciliation: trust, commitment, and emotional healing. I then focus on apology and imagination as two elements that help to create this foundation. The chapter ends with practical ways to reconcile, including how to connect while establishing healthy boundaries.

Reconciliation: Building a Foundation

I believe that *all communication is reconciliation*. Because of the natural flux of relationships, every time we connect with a relational partner, we are really re-connecting. In essence we are in a constant state of reconciling (reuniting, retuning) with one another. Viewing relationships this way helps protect us from taking our relationships for granted because we see them as static, nonchanging. Instead we can approach each new meeting with a relationship partner with expectation— How will my partner and I reconnect tonight when she returns home from work? What will it be like to be with my son, who lives out of state, again? How wonderful to discover new things with my friend tonight as we hang out together.

Yet, reconciliation is a complex, multifaceted process when it occurs after a relationship transgression. As we saw in the opening examples, reconciliation takes various forms and manifests itself at different levels, from full restoration to casual periodic contact. In fact, my early forgiveness work (Kelley, 1998) demonstrated that relational outcomes post-transgression, even with forgiveness, vary significantly. Some relationships return to their previous state. Some relationships actually strengthen as individuals renegotiate their relational partnerships. Other relationships weaken or eventually terminate, partners unable to manage the disruption of the transgression. And, some relationships continue, but take on a different form. For instance, dating couples may terminate their dating relationship, but continue to be friends because they are part of the same social circles. In the same way, divorced couples with children and grandchildren often maintain some level of reconciliation until one of them dies.

Trust and Commitment

The various manifestations of reconciliation are based on the ability and willingness of partners to reestablish commitment and restore trust in the relationship. As we saw in the previous chapter, Chapter Twelve: "Forgiveness: Choosing How You Want to Live," relationship hurt often comes from transgression and some type of personal devaluation. These hurtful experiences reorient our attention to our partner and whether she is available and responsive to us. Essentially, is she committed and trustworthy in the relationship?

Rusbult, Hannon, Stocker, and Finkel (2005) define commitment as the "extent to which each partner intends to persist in the relationship, feels psychologically attached to it, and exhibits long-term orientation toward it" (p. 187). Essentially, commitment is assurance from one's partner that he will work for *my* good, and *our* good, for an indefinite period of time. The driving force of commitment is trust. There is no way to guarantee trust in a relationship, but commitment to one another's well-being is a good place to start (see Chapter Four: "Love Relationships"). As Rusbult et al. (2005) put it, "trust represents conviction regarding the strength of a partner's commitment" (p. 187).

Trust is essential to reestablishing interdependence and intimacy in broken relationships. In essence, if we are to *create a space where if something good can happen, it will*, then we must create a space characterized by growing levels of trust. To paraphrase communication scholar Bill Wilmot—Have you noticed how wonderfully people change when they feel safe? A place where something good can happen is a safe space. It is a space where I trust that my well-being is paramount. It is in the arms of trust that I am free to change.

How do we create that safe space? One way is to state your commitment to your partner—"I've got your back," "You know I'll be here for you," "It turns me on to think of growing old together." But, as necessary as the words are, they only have power when they are supported by patterns of trustworthy behavior. Worthington and Drinkard (2000) emphasize that trust is restored through "mutual trustworthy behavior" (p. 93). When my son, Daniel, went through an extended rebellious period in high school, but was trying to turn his life around, at one point he said, "You don't trust me." I answered, "I trust your motives. I just don't trust that if you get caught in the 'wrong' situation, you'll do the 'right' thing." The bottom line is that simply wanting to do something doesn't guarantee that you are actually going to do it. Your abusive partner might genuinely want to change his behavior, but until you see changed behavior over an extended period of time, you should be careful to give him your full trust.

Hargrave and Sells (1997) believe that trustworthiness, at its very core, is related to how justice is expressed relationally:

> When people engage in relationships that have a balance of give (obligations) and take (entitlements) over a period of time, the innate sense of justice is satisfied and trustworthiness is established in the relationship. However, when there is a consistent or severe imbalance between the relational give and take, the sense of justice is violated and individuals feel cheated or overbenefited by the relationship. . . .. The work of forgiveness . . . is defined as effort in restoring love and trustworthiness to relationships.
>
> *(pp. 42–43)*

Hargrave and Sells emphasize that just behavior (equity between give and take) creates trust in the relationship. *Just relationships are trust relationships.* However, when trust has been broken though an imbalance in the relationship it has to be reestablished in order to restore intimacy. The means to accomplish this, according to Hargrave and Sells, is forgiveness. In Chapter Twelve: "Forgiveness: Choosing How You Want to Live," I discuss forgiveness as creating opportunity for reconciliation because, through forgiveness, you can begin healing your emotions and, subsequently, reconstitute commitment and trust in the relationship. Without this emotional healing we tend to cut ourselves off emotionally from our relational partner, are hesitant to trust, lack resilience and the ability to engage conflict constructively, possibly engage in cycles of rumination and punitive behavior, and likely dehumanize the other person.

Emotional Healing

Previous work of mine (Kelley, 2012) blends Gordon and Baucom's (1999, 2003) forgiveness model (based on research with couples who have endured infidelity) and Waldron's and my tasks of forgiveness (2008) into four stages that provide a framework for understanding how emotional healing takes place. *Managing the impact* entails a great deal of emotion work as it involves handling the couples' initial response to revelation of the transgression. This time is typically characterized by uncertainty, anger, hurt, and fear in light of an increasing sense of numbness, disbelief, and risk. A key motivation early on is to restore well-being. Although it is impossible at this stage to restore well-being completely, the goal is to manage one's emotional experience enough that one can avoid regretful decisions that come in the midst of overwhelming pain. Healthily managing one's emotions, during this first stage, may include identifying one's emotional experience and expressing emotions in a safe context (counseling, a good friend, journaling). Critical behaviors at this time are setting appropriate boundaries, beginning self-care, and managing emotions.

The second stage, *making sense of one's self, partner, and relationship*, can positively affect the partners' emotional experience by increasing understanding of others and the event. As increased understanding leads to learning, positive impact (e.g., psychological or spiritual growth), and rethinking one's own identity, the debilitating effect of one's negative emotional response lessens, providing positive motivation to move forward in the process and avoid being stuck in a cycle of negative thinking and emotion.

Engaging forgiveness is the third stage. Here, partners' hard emotions dissipate, along with their desire for revenge or "perfect justice," and they begin to integrate the soft emotions of hurt and sadness with more positive emotional experiences. Behavior during this time shifts significantly and is characterized by nondefensive listening, apology, nonverbal displays of sincerity, and empathy.

The final stage, *negotiating reconciliation*, is characterized by genuine dialogue. The healthy emotion work that has been done up to this point enables the couple to reasonably engage one another and make healthy choices about the possible continuance of the relationship. If the relationship continues, key tasks are to reestablish intimacy levels and the relationship's moral order.

Full reconciliation, as opposed to "quick fix" reconciliation characterized by a simple apology, involves the transcendent synthesis of both positive and negative emotions. Malcolm, Warwar, and Greenberg (2005) describe this process as "occurring when opposing emotions are co-activated and new, higher level schemes are formed that incorporate both emotions" (p. 384). The goal of forgiveness is not to stuff negative emotions and muster up positive ones, and the goal of reconciliation is not to ignore negative emotions in order to achieve low-level reconnection. Rather, forgiveness and reconciliation involve a somewhat paradoxical holding of both negative and positive—"It still hurts to think of what you did, but I love you and want to trust you and rebuild our relationship." (Note: because the process of emotional integration makes one emotionally vulnerable, please engage this emotional work where conditions are safe, e.g., with a counselor, mentor, or good friend).

Apology

Apology is a means of creating a safe place for reconciliation (Kelley, 2012). When speaking about forgiveness and reconciliation I am frequently asked about whether or not the offending party needs to apologize. The short answer is: for forgiveness, no; for full reconciliation, yes. Because forgiveness can take place at an individual, psychological level, I don't want to be dependent on another person's action (e.g., apology) to determine whether I can forgive. Being dependent on my offender's response to be free from my own negative emotions keeps me under her control. Therefore, I am *not dependent* on her apology to forgive. However, regarding reconciliation, I am *free* to set boundaries that create a *just relationship*. Because reconciliation is about creating a safe space where two individuals can reunite as friends, lovers, family, or neighbors, apology can be crucial to demonstrating remorse, an understanding of the past, and hope for a just future.

Many of us learned to apologize by simply saying, "I am sorry." No emotion. Forced to say it by Mom, or because the other person was going to take away an important resource ("If you don't say you're sorry, you can't use my iPhone."). However, full apologies create a positive setting for reconciliation because they include a variety of elements missed by our perfunctory "sorry." Full apologies include a recognition of the wrong done. Not just a general acknowledgement that the other person was hurt, but a specific identification of how the other person was hurt ("I know it was a hassle to find your car without gas, but I think what really bothered you was that I didn't at least send you a text telling you that I left it without gas."). Full apologies must be viewed as sincere, thus, they are often accompanied by nonverbal shows of empathy and remorse for the hurt partner. And, finally, full apologies are future oriented, including a promise of restitution, when appropriate ("Next time we're out, I owe you a full tank of gas!") and specifically detailing what will change so that the offense will not happen again. In this sense, full apologies create spaces where partners once again commit to and trust one another.

Before moving on, I should note that apology is very difficult for many people. As such, full reconciliation may occur without apology as long as the elements of apology are in some way evident—creating a space for commitment and trust. In our study of long-term couples a number of wives mentioned that their husbands had trouble apologizing, or apologizing first. Yet, they were confident in their husbands' commitment to them and remorse over their choices and behavior.

Imagining the Future

I finish this section by returning to imagination. In Chapter Seven: "Dehumanizing the 'Other'", I introduced you to thinking by Honeycutt (2008) who suggests that imagined interactions can have significant effects on our relationships. Later, I introduced you to Oelofson (2009), who believes that we can rehumanize others by using our imaginations to empathize. By using our imagination we see others' problems and pains, external contingencies and internal limitations.

But imagination grants us something else, as well. Imagination gives us hope. Imagination allows us to creatively engage the future. Not blindly, but in dialogue with those with whom we share our lives (Oelofson, 2009). As Tint (2010) states, "Dialogue is a practical manifestation of this concept of encounter and provides the link in the present between past and future" (p. 274). Genuine dialogue (Chapter Three: "Good Relationships") connects us with the others in our lives. When we are in genuine dialogue with others we are present, together. And when we are present together, we are human together. And, when we are human together, we can imagine a just future together.

WHERE IS HE AT, I FORGIVEN U

by Shanae G.

> Gone when I was 3
> Left with no memories
> Cherished by thoughts
> Isolated my hope
> Where did my dad go?
> I guess I'll never know
> Looking at time
> Wondering when
> He'll walk through that door again
> I'll never say it like I used to
> The word I love you start to confuse u
> Hated your mistake
> Missing my birthday
> Never thought I would forgive you
> Caught me at the end
> Now it's been enough time to forgive
> As time starts over you never missed a birthday again
> Calling you dad is the weirdest thing I've did
> Saying it in person will be a feeling unknown
> But saying your name is joy in my head
> Because I could tell you Joe Jackson I love you again.

Shanae's own commentary: I always felt that my father was no one to me. I had all these emotions built up about how he missed my birthday and I didn't get a card in the mail. However, once we connected again I just couldn't call him dad; I called him by his real name. I felt that because I haven't seen him or known what it feels like to have a dad figure, why do I want to tell him *I love you* or give him the privilege to be called "Dad" again. I have forgiven you and thank you for allowing me to express every emotion or problem I have with you.

Reconciling Relationships

Reconciliation involves emotional healing from relationship trauma, and the subsequent development of commitment and trust. Worthington (Worthington, 2006; Worthington & Drinkard, 2000) conceptualizes reconciliation as maintaining intimacy, and uses a bridge metaphor to discuss reconciliation with couples. Using his approach as a guide, I present six charges for relational partners who choose to connect or reconnect. I discuss these six elements as "charges," because, although it is tempting to think reconciliation follows a linear sequence, often partners are working on multiple charges simultaneously.

The first charge is to *commit to exploring reconciliation*. Some make this decision because cultural values (e.g., "We don't believe in divorce") dictate the response. For others, internal values (e.g., "No one gets away with cheating on me") guide the process. However, internal and external values shift during actual interactions, and the decision regarding reconciliation has to be worked out over time. That is why partners commit to *exploring* reconciliation. And, as I've mentioned in previous chapters, if emotional and physical safety are ever in question, either partner can stop the process.

The second charge is to *rehumanize the other*. Empathy and understanding of our partner's past and personal limitations help with this step. We become more open when we view our partners as imperfect human beings with imperfect pasts and, as such, begin to shift our relationship frame. Third, we *choose to heal our emotional pain*. As our negative emotions become increasingly integrated with positive emotions (e.g., my anger being combined with compassion for you), I may be able to resist my tight hold on the negative experience and work toward full forgiveness and reconciliation.

We have a fourth charge that permeates the reconciliation process—*rebuild broken trust*. The emotions associated with broken trust are likely being dealt with as part of all of the charges. However, rebuilding broken trust involves setting appropriate boundaries (discussed later) while allowing your partner to demonstrate that they truly intend to be, and can be, trustworthy. As our negative emotions subside and we begin to rebuild trust, we are able to slow unproductive, mindless patterns (e.g., defensiveness) and replace them with *new, positive patterns*—this is our fifth charge. In other words, we disrupt the negative patterns that have developed—especially negative reciprocity and emotional distancing – but this time, we stay engaged and respond to defensiveness, and any additional attacks, in new ways (mindfulness) that do not escalate the conflict or create emotional distance. Over time, these new patterns will maintain the reconciliation (positive mindless patterns). For instance, when a partner says something with a negative tone, we can make our new habit to ask an open-ended question—"Are you upset about something?"

The final charge is, *commit to love and personal advocacy*. Part I of this book ends with the assertion that love and advocacy create just relationships. Love, which includes commitment, is the context and means for long-term justice. Advocacy creates a safe space for new creation of the relationship, and the growth and affirmation of each individual partner. If choosing love and advocacy sounds weak, like you are becoming the doormat of the relationship, remember that the first reconciliation charge involves assessing the emotional and physical safety of the relationship. Also, recognize that a truly loving response that advocates for the well-being of both partners may be to set appropriate boundaries or end the relationship.

> *Living It Out: Think about a relationship you are in that has not been fully reconciled. Go through each of the six prescribed charges and assess where you are in the process of reconciliation. Do you want to move forward? Is it safe to move forward? Using the six charges, how can you move forward?*
>
> *Living It Out: Is there a way for you to increase your commitment to the process of reconciliation, or further build trust?*

Apology

We've discussed four essential elements to full apology. First the person who hurt you needs to recognize, with good insight, why the transgression or personal injury was hurtful. Second, the offender needs to show that they sincerely feel remorse for pain he has caused. Third, he must offer restitution, if appropriate. Fourth, he must demonstrate how life is going to be different—how is he going to change things to minimize the chance of hurting you this way again?

> *Living It Out: Has the person who hurt you apologized? If so, do you think he or she is sincere? Do you think they really understand the core of what hurt you? If not, can you talk to him or her about these elements?*
>
> *Living It Out: If apology is difficult for the person who hurt you, but you still want to reconcile, do you think he or she is remorseful and committed to rebuilding trust?*

Setting Boundaries in Love

As we have been discussing throughout this book, and especially in this chapter, just relationships are relationships that are fair for your partner . . . and, you! That often means setting healthy boundaries. Boundaries can be set wherever you feel vulnerable: physical, sexual, intellectual, emotional, spiritual. I have been teaching about boundaries for years using the following imagery. Palm side up, hold out your left hand toward the person who hurt you. Tell her something like—"I love you. I care for you. I would like to be in relationship with you." Now, palm side up, hold out your right hand, parallel to the left. Tell her something like—"Certain things are good for me, and certain things are harmful. I have decided to live in a way that is best for me. I need you to respect my choice. If you can't, then I can't be in relationship with you right now (or, I can only be in relationship with you in a certain way [like, only at family gatherings])." The open palms represent an openness to rebuilding the relationship. They signal that you are approachable and safe. At the same time, they firmly present parallel paths. One path is love and connection—I want a relationship with you. The other side is justice and respect—I can only be in relationship with you in certain fair and respectful ways.

As a final note regarding boundaries, be careful making your love or forgiveness conditional. In our research, conditional forgiveness (I will forgive you if . . .") has been associated with deteriorating relationships, possibly because it is unilateral and signals a lack of trust (Waldron & Kelley, 2008).

> *Living It Out: Are you currently in a relationship with someone with whom you need to set boundaries? If so, how can you communicate sincerely that you would like a relationship with him or her? How can you set boundaries that are good for you, but do it in a way that isn't a power play or making your forgiveness conditional?*

Imagination

Several times in our journey toward creating *just relationships* we have discussed imagination. Imagination is not about being unrealistic. It is actually about being most realistic. Without imagination we stay locked into our limited worldviews, our relationship frames narrow revealing only one perspective on our relationships and our partners. Imagination, on the other hand, sheds light on the world from a variety of vantage points. Most specifically, it allows us to see from other persons' perspectives (new relationship frames), and think creatively about how to generate new, just relationships. Imagination, as it is tied to reconciliation, facilitates connection between once separated parties and, generously, imparts hope for the future.

> *Living It Out: Choose a relational partner with whom you have had some difficulty. Imagine what her childhood was like. Imagine being in some of the relationships she has experienced. Let your mind help you to see her as an imperfect person who is doing her best to survive, to find love, to find intimacy.*
>
> *Living It Out: Without sharing this part with your partner, imagine your "perfect" future with her. Now, take that future and break it down to better understand what you are really looking for in a partner, in your joint future. Are you able to share these hopes and desires with your partner and see if there is reason to reconcile?*

Case 13.1

Lori is 23 years old and has never known her biological dad. He left when she was 18 months old and never contacted her or her older sister. When she was young, she would ask her mom about "Daddy," and was gently, but sternly, told to never call him that—"He abandoned us." Lori's mom soon remarried and Lori's new stepdad, Kevin, always showed Lori and her sister great love and support. Lori grew to deeply love Kevin and called him "Dad." She covered up lingering pain, regarding her biological father, by only referring to him as "sperm donor."

Lori is engaged to Jay and they are to be married in a month. Out of the blue, two weeks ago, Lori received a friend request on Facebook from her biological father. She immediately contacted Jay and told him her "sperm donor" had contacted her, and they talked about her father's friend request for a week. Finally she decided that she could unfriend him if things didn't go well, so she clicked "confirm." Within an hour, her newest Facebook friend had messaged her with an apology for leaving her all those years ago, and asking if they could meet and talk. Lori was flooded with mixed emotions. Again, she and Jay talked, and they decided it would be okay to meet as long as it was in a public space and for a fixed period of time. Two days later Lori met her "sperm donor" at The Brew Coffeehouse.

After the meeting with her dad, Lori processed with Jay. Things had started out really awkwardly, but her dad actually seemed like a nice person. He apologized, again, for having left when she was so little, and reiterated how badly he felt—he told her that he was just immature and full of fear as a young man. He heard from a friend that she was getting married and something inside him just "clicked." He knew then and there that he wanted to know his daughter and wondered if he could come to the wedding. Lori was taken aback at his request. She was filled with mixed emotions, but didn't want him to see her upset, so she just told him she would have to think about it and that she had to go. On the way out the door, her dad continued his efforts by telling her that he would like to know his grandkids, when the time came for that, and promised he would be there for them. Lori's head was reeling as she sat in her car and watched him drive away. She wasn't sure why, but she just began to cry. As she talked things over with Jay, she realized that her dad had apologized and seemed sincere enough. But it all was so sudden and she didn't really know him at all, and it felt like a huge emotional risk to let him into her life. Why did he have to complicate things right before the wedding?

Processing

1. Describe the foundational elements of reconciliation (commitment, trust, emotional healing) that are present, or missing, from this situation.
2. How would you rate Lori's dad's apology? Rewrite his apology in a way that might help Lori be open to reconciliation.
3. Which of the six reconciliation charges do you think will require the most work if Lori decides to reconcile with her biological father?
4. Suppose Lori and her biological father are to meet again. Help Lori set healthy boundaries with him.

Case 13.2

Tyrone grew up in New York City with his mom, dad, and two brothers. His family was financially well off, and both parents were college-educated and held professional jobs.

They were proud of their African-American heritage. Tyrone was an easygoing child—he played some sports, went to church with his family, hung out with his friends. He attended a private school with his brothers, and his friends were racially mixed.

As the middle child, Tyrone had often felt different than his brothers—he was good at sports, but less invested in it; he liked girls, enough, but never really dated. In his first year of college he found himself with friends at a gay bar. It was fun, but it also put him in touch with certain feelings he'd never let himself experience. Nothing "happened" that night, but it started a two-year process whereby Tyrone concluded that he might be gay. Because Tyrone was primarily focused on his grades, none of this mattered much to him until his senior year when he met someone that he wanted to date. One day he got a phone call from one of his brothers, "Ty, I saw your pictures on Instagram. We have to talk."

Ty's brother, Cedric, asked him straight up, "Are you dating a guy?" Ty was confused by Cedric's intensity. "I don't know. We're just hanging out a lot." Cedric continued, "Well you better know, because I got a call from Dad and he wants me to find out. If you are, he told me you are not welcome at home for Thanksgiving." Ty had heard his dad make jokes about gay people, but it never occurred to him that his dad felt this strongly about things. Ty tried calling his dad, but his dad didn't answer the phone, he just texted back: "I talked with Cedric and saw the pictures, and that's enough for me. You can either choose to be part of this family, or not." In the heat of the anger and hurt generated from his dad's text, Ty texted back, "*NOT!*" It has been three years since Ty has been home or talked to his dad. He has not been in a "relationship" and is still thinking through his sexual identity. But, one thing he knows for sure: "I am not choosing my sexual identity based on what my dad wants."

Ty's family did not attend his college graduation, and now he is finishing his master's degree and they are not planning to come. Cedric knows his dad is proud of Ty, even though he won't say it out loud, and he knows that Ty misses his family. To resolve things, Cedric has invited his family and Ty (without either knowing the other is coming) to his daughter's first birthday party. He hopes that with his daughter as the focus, he can begin to help Ty and his dad reconcile.

Processing

1. Describe the foundational elements of reconciliation (commitment, trust, emotional healing) that are present, or missing, from this situation.
2. Using the six reconciliation charges, help Cedric think through how his dad and Ty can begin to work on reconciling.
3. How might imagination help Ty's dad better understand Ty's search for his own sexual identity?

References

Gordon, K. C., & Baucom, D. H. (1999). A multitheoretical intervention for promoting recovery from extramarital affairs. *Clinical Psychology: Science and Practice, 6*, 382–399.

Gordon, K. C., & Baucom, D. H. (2003). Understanding betrayals in marriage: A synthesized model of forgiveness. *Family Process, 37*, 425–449.

Hargrave, T. D., & Sells, J. N. (1997). The development of a forgiveness scale. *Journal of Marital and Family Therapy, 23*, 41–62.

Honeycutt, J. M. (2008). Imagined interaction theory. In L. A. Baxter & D. O. Braithwaite (Eds.), *Engaging theories in interpersonal communication: Multiple perspectives* (pp. 77–88). Thousand Oaks: Sage.

Kelley, D. L. (1998). The communication of forgiveness. *Communication Studies, 49*, 255–271.

Kelley, D. L. (2012). Forgiveness as restoration: The search for well-being, reconciliation, and relational justice. In T. J. Socha & M. J. Pitts (Eds.), *The positive side of interpersonal communication* (pp. 193–209). New York: Peter Lang.

Malcolm, W., Warwar, S., & Greenberg, L. (2005). Facilitating forgiveness in individual therapy as an approach to resolving interpersonal injuries. In E. L. Worthington, Jr. (Ed.), *Handbook of forgiveness* (pp. 379–391). New York: Routledge.

Oelofsen, R. (2009). De- and rehumanization in the wake of atrocities. *South African Journal of Philosophy, 28*(2), 178–188.

Rusbult, C. E., Hannon, P. A., Stocker, S. L., & Finkel, E. J. (2005). Forgiveness and relational repair. In E. L. Worthington, Jr. (Ed.), *Handbook of forgiveness* (pp. 185–206). New York: Routledge.

Tint, B. S. (2010). Dialogue, forgiveness, and reconciliation. In A. Kalayjian & R. F. Paloutzian (Eds.), *Forgiveness and reconciliation: Psychological pathways to conflict transformation and peace building* (pp. 269–285). New York: Springer.

Waldron, V. R., & Kelley, D. L. (2008). *Communicating forgiveness*. Thousand Oaks, CA: Sage.

Worthington, E. L. Jr. (2006). *Forgiveness and reconciliation: Theory and application*. New York: Routledge.

Worthington, E. L., & Drinkard, D. T. (2000). Promoting reconciliation through psycho-educational and therapeutic interventions. *Journal of Marital and Family Therapy, 26*, 93–101.

PART IV

Just Musings

I like the idea of musings. Steven Pressfield in his book, *The War of Art*, suggests that we make spaces for the muses in our lives. He uses the term "muses" to describe the "psychic forces that support and sustain us in our journey toward ourselves" (2012, p. 106). You probably didn't think much about my own personal journey as you read this book—but writing *Just Relationships* has been a significant part of my journey. As I write these words, I've just finished a "fresh read" of the manuscript, making final changes for the Routledge staff. Such joy! in rediscovering the good things that are packed in this small volume. This is an important book that I hope you will take time to ponder, and chew upon—take time for your own muses to show up. For me, as I read each section, I realized there were issues in *Living It Out* that I still need to work into my life. Also, many of the themes that have been on my heart for the past 20-plus years of teaching stood out more clearly to me. As we close our time together, let me highlight a few of those themes for you.

I'm definitely a grace guy. Years ago when running residence halls at Whitworth College my colleagues joked that my first book would be titled *Grace Abounds*. They were kidding of course, but I make no apologies for loving the ideas of grace and mercy. It was these loves that directed me toward the study of forgiveness and, unexpectedly, highlighted the need for people to experience *justice* in their lives. Yet, watching people's justice attempts has generally left me disappointed and, at times, appalled. The result of these realizations is *Part I: Imagining Just Relationships: Perspectives*, four chapters that have blended the ideas of justice, morality, love, and advocacy to reflect a less dualistic way of seeing life.

What do I mean by "less dualistic"? In my counseling training I was very much intrigued by *gestalt* therapeutic approaches. Gestalt essentially means whole—a whole that is more than the sum of its parts. As such, gestalt therapists tend to see things as connected. That's me. While I believe in embracing differences, I am committed to the idea that this best happens when we see our connectedness, and when we endeavor to make sure that the differences we embrace do not create false distinctions between us.

In this light, I hope it is clear that I very much believe that justice is related to creating spaces where we embrace our full humanity, where we each become complete persons living in just, loving communities. Love, advocacy, forgiveness, and reconciliation all move us toward these end goals—each a distinct means, but all pointed toward the same end.

The process of creating *just relationships* involves awareness of both self and others. As you read each chapter, you may have been surprised at how often I asked you to look at your own behavior, worldview or relationship frame, and identity. I am troubled at how we dehumanize each other, and ourselves. In my own life I have seen too many adults in bondage over the shame they have buried deep inside. As I have often said to my students, "Healthy relationships are built on healthy people" (see Kim, 2012). Healthy people are resilient, positively engage conflict, take responsibility for their actions, empathize, are creative, and humanize themselves and others. As such, our journey toward healthy, *just relationships* is very much a journey of self-discovery, choosing to reframe our thinking and heal our emotional baggage.

On the other hand, we won't get very far in creating the relationships we want if we don't understand one another. Over and again I reference the ideas of dialogue, mindfulness, empathy, imagination, framing, and boundaries. These practices create safe spaces for being and becoming. In many respects, they represent moral ways of joining with others. I love the ideas of imagination and play as creative ways of engaging other persons. Likewise, a favorite phrase, *create a space where if something good can happen, it will*, signifies for me that I can take action, but I am also not in complete control of any given situation or person. There is wonderful freedom in this perspective—freedom to act, and freedom not to be bound by others' response.

It is my hope that this book has been *a safe space* for you, *where if something good can happen it will*. Now, go, invite others into a co-creation of the world in which we live.

I

I thought I saw you,
But I only saw my own reflection.
I thought you were free,
But I didn't understand where you came from.
I talked at you,
But I never met you.
I spoke of you,
But I never knew you.
I never knew me.

Doug

References

Kim, Y. Y. (2012). Being in concert: An explication of synchrony in positive intercultural communication. In T. Socha & M. Pitts (Eds.), *The positive side of interpersonal communication* (pp. 39–56). New York: Peter Lang.

Pressfield, S. (2012). *The war of art*. New York: Black Irish Entertainment LLC.

INDEX

abuse 98, 104, 120

accounts 79

adaptability 47, 71, 72, 98, 102

advocacy 5, 40–8, 56, 58, 123, 134–5, 141–2

apology 64, 78–9, 85, 103, 124, 129, 131, 132, 135, 137, 141

arousal 6, 22, 106, 108–9, 111–12, 114, 120

attachment Theory 4, 57, 58, 62–3, 65, 118, 117

attribution Theory xiv, 4, 57, 60, 63, 70, 86, 93, 100; attributions 15, 79, 87

avoidance 79–81, 86

balance 5–6, 9, 12, 14, 16, 81, 106–12, 123, 130; imbalance 4, 115

blame 58, 79, 83, 85–90, 93, 111, 114, 123

boundaries 6, 23, 103, 110, 119, 129, 131–2, 134–6, 142

co-create 12, 42, 56, 61, 71, 116

commitment 6, 12, 14, 32–7, 123, 128–30, 132, 134–5, 137–8

defensiveness 26, 34, 36, 73, 80–1, 85–90, 108, 112, 131, 154

dehumanization 5, 67–70, 72–5, 87, 130, 142

dialogue 5, 13, 15, 21–8, 42–3, 45, 56, 58, 64, 70, 73, 77, 81–3, 90, 106, 111–12, 116, 131, 133, 142

distress-maintaining 60–1, 63, 65–6, 70, 90; *see also* relationship-enhancing attributions

distributive justice 10, 12, 14, 17–18

early recollections 63

emotional bonding 33–7

emotional healing 6, 119, 129–31, 134, 137–8

emotions, hard and soft 119–20, 131

empathy 15, 19–20, 70–1, 73, 80, 90–2, 120, 122, 131–2, 134, 142

equality xiv, 3–5, 9–18, 21–2, 25, 30–1, 33, 45, 58, 67–70, 72, 76, 109–10, 112, 119, 121, 123, 125, 128

equity xiv, xv, 3–4, 7, 9–18, 38, 58, 106, 109, 116, 130

Equity Theory 4

ethnocentrism 69–73

face 6, 42, 76–83, 99–100, 119, 125

facework 77–80, 83, 85, 109

fair 3–6, 9–17, 20, 22, 30, 36, 38, 41, 58, 76, 78, 87, 90, 101, 106, 109, 117, 121, 135–6

forgiveness 4, 6–7, 10, 20–2, 33, 69, 79, 81, 99, 116–26, 128–34, 136, 141–2; Hand of Forgiveness 123–4; tasks of forgiveness 131; TUF Forgiveness 122–3

full love 30, 32–4, 37–8, 43

goals of interaction 77–8, 108–9, 120

guilt 77–8, 86–94, 114, 124

heal 116, 122, 134, 142
homeostasis 107
humor 22, 69, 79, 98
hurt 3, 6, 9–11, 15, 20–1, 30–1, 35, 41,
    61, 63, 65, 71, 74, 77, 79, 82–3, 85–6,
    88, 92, 101, 108, 116–25, 129, 131–2,
    135, 138

identity 4–5, 11, 42, 69, 71–2, 77–81, 91,
    99–100, 102, 108–9, 131, 138, 142
imagination 5–6, 56, 69–73, 75, 129,
    132–3, 136, 138, 142
Imagined Interaction Theory 139
infrahumanization 68–9, 71–2, 75
intimacy 14, 30–3, 37, 58, 130–1, 136

justice motive 10, 118

mentor 10, 21, 27, 40–50, 75, 122,
    124, 131
mercy 27, 117–19, 141
mindfulness 23–4, 26, 28, 43, 45, 47,
    49–50, 73, 90–1, 98, 107, 111,
    134, 142
mindlessness 6, 106–8, 111, 114, 134
morality 4–5, 20–3, 68, 141
mutuality 45, 49–50

Negotiated Morality Theory 20–2
negotiation 5, 10, 12–13, 16, 19–26, 77,
    88, 109–10, 118, 120–1, 129, 131
nonviolence 12, 15–16

ordinary magic 97
other-centeredness 25, 33–4, 36, 58, 73

pain 10–11, 20, 31, 68, 70, 73–4, 89,
    116–18, 121–2, 125–6, 128, 131–7
peer support 43, 45, 49, 56
play 47–50, 69, 142
power 3–4, 6, 26, 31, 43, 88, 106–7,
    109–15, 118–19, 136
power balancing 110, 112
processual justice 11–15, 22, 30, 79
promise 20, 33, 132, 137
protective factors 6, 98, 101–2

reconciliation 4, 6, 22, 89, 118, 120–1,
    128–38, 142
Relational Framing Theory 57, 62

relational justice 9–10, 14, 22, 30
relationship-enhancing attributions
    60–1, 63, 65–6, 70, 90; *see also*
    distress-maintaining
relationship frame (framing) 55–66, 67–73,
    86, 90, 100–1, 117, 134, 136, 142
relationship messages 108–9
repair 79, 88, 117
resilience 6, 91–4, 97–104, 106, 112, 116,
    118, 130, 142
respect 3, 5–6, 10–12, 14–16, 18, 20, 22,
    24, 27–8, 30–2, 34, 36, 58, 60–1, 67,
    72, 74, 78–9, 81, 92, 112, 119, 123,
    135–6
responsibility 23, 28, 35, 41, 79, 86–91,
    117, 142
restorative justice 88–91
risk 6, 10, 30–3, 43, 97–8, 101–4

safe space 6, 22, 26, 32–3, 36, 40, 42,
    47–8, 73, 130, 132, 135, 142
self-advocacy 43
self-awareness 47, 71, 80
self-efficacy 3, 98
self-sacrifice 33, 37, 43; *see also*
    other-centeredness
shame 6–7, 68, 85–94, 142
shame resilience 91–4
social justice 3–5, 9, 19, 23, 30, 32–3, 56,
    58, 106, 109
social support 21, 74, 98, 100, 102,
    110, 112

transcendence 91, 106, 111–15, 131
tribe 62, 67, 70–1
trust 6, 12, 21, 31, 33, 35, 46, 48, 58, 61,
    63–6, 93, 112, 119, 123, 128–38
truth 15, 20, 44, 121–2, 125–6
TUF Forgiveness *see* forgiveness

Ubuntu 33–4, 36, 42, 45, 106
understanding 10, 12–13, 20, 26, 41, 45,
    47, 56, 58, 62, 71–4, 79, 90, 119, 122,
    126, 131–2, 134

voice 11, 24, 27, 40–5, 109, 113, 120, 122
vulnerability 30–3, 37–8, 73, 112, 117,
    120, 122–4, 131

worldview 5, 12, 49, 55–67, 69, 99, 136, 142